Energize Your Heart

in Four Dimensions

by Puran and Susanna Bair

Living Heart Media
Tucson, AZ

Energize Your Heart In Four Dimensions

Living Heart Media
PO Box 86149
Tucson AZ 85754
www.livingheartmedia.com

First edition

Printed in the United States of America

Edition ISBNs:

Softcover	978-0-9795269-1-6
Audio	978-0-9795269-4-7
E-Book	978-0-9795269-3-0

Library of Congress Control Number – 2007929623

Peggy Walsh

What people are saying about *Energize Your Heart* and Heart Rhythm Meditation

Puran and Susanna Bair are Masters of our time. In sharing their wisdom, they take you on an exquisite journey into the vast expanse of the heart. I daresay that no one has previously come close to the level of discernment and differentiation presented here - in understanding what is exactly at stake and in inspiring the reader with what can be mastered and attained by adopting their incredibly empowering method of Heart Rhythm Meditation. The greatness of wisdom in this volume is life-changing.

Howard Glasser, Author, *Transforming the Difficult Child* and *All Children Flourishing*

Over the years, *Living from the Heart* by Puran Bair is the one book I have recommended more than any other. This second contribution from the Bairs extends and deepens the practical wisdom they have gleaned from years of teaching and exploration into the endless mystery of the heart. You will find science, poetry and inspiration, and much more, in these pages. I know this book will forever enhance the meaning and enjoyment of your life.

Dr. James L. Oschman, Author, *Energy Medicine: The Scientific Basis*

This unique book reveals information about the heart that is innovative, inspiring and applicable. Though drawing upon ancient sources of wisdom, the Bairs provide insights valuable to modern people right in the midst of our everyday joys and challenges. *Energize Your Heart* not only convinces us that cultivating our mystical heart is possible amidst the obligations of family, friendships and livelihoods – it also lays out an elegant framework for fully developing the innate qualities that lie in the heart of each one of us. Practices such as these will build the heart-centered culture, founded on peace and respect, that we seek for ourselves, our children, grandchildren and for all life.

Dr. Bonnie Colby, University of Arizona

Every person who reads this book will benefit. This luminous book is an extremely practical, powerful guide to the path of heart. It's clear, lucid language evokes each feeling of the heart as its dimensions are described. The authors provide a step-by-step method for defining and expanding the breadth, height, depth, driving force, and inner dimension of the heart. From the initial description of the physical heart and heart center to realms of the spiritual heart, a picture of the whole heart comes together, lending an intuitive understanding of our relation to all of humanity.

Dr. Patricia Norris, pioneering psychoneuroimmunologist and professor, Holos University Graduate Seminary

I've used HRM to lower my blood pressure to the point of reducing the medication I take for it, stave off migraine headaches, and to quiet heart arrhythmia when I'm stressed or overtired. Emotionally, I was able to come through a very difficult marital breakdown and negotiate a win-win divorce without the intervention of attorneys. I've healed many childhood wounds, and restored optimism to my life. I feel a deep sense of peace, harmony and gratitude now that I've been able to find my life's work, and a deeper connection to my faith than I've ever had at any time of my life.

Ronnie Howell, BA

I feel that Heart Rhythm Meditation has saved my life, prevented a heart attack and stroke, as I am diabetic with high blood pressure and 57 years old. After each Heart Rhythm session I feel calmer and rejuvenated. It has always worked and I am very grateful for its impact in my life. I know that it has helped me with stress at work, and it has saved my relationships with my students and girlfriend many times beyond measure. It has provided me with a new lease on life, a more complete and fulfilled perspective on what life and living is all about, and a greater ability to be more productive and functional in my average daily life.

Jim Cumming, MS, MA, teacher, former Army captain

Soon after being introduced to HRM and applying the meditation practices, my blood pressure began coming down, I became more accepting of myself and I literally found my heart! HRM opened my heart letting 50 years of emotion flow making my life more alive and real! I have a much clearer picture of who I am, what makes me tick, and live more from an open and accepting heart.

Porter Underwood, Petroleum consultant

Over the years I have practiced HRM, there have been profound shifts in my life. As a classical musician, I have greater ease of playing, creativity in expression, and higher concentration levels than ever before. My relationships with colleagues, friends and family have never been better or had the richness and depth of intimacy that they now have. My health is great.

Robert Johnson, Assistant principal, Lyric Opera of Chicago

The forgiveness and gratitude practices of Heart Rhythm Practice have been gifts beyond price, allowing me to open to my life now with so much gratefulness. It's like being able to breathe fully for the first time.

Jody Curley, MA, CBOT

I had elevated blood pressure for several years and was on medication for this. Even with medication my blood pressure would still occasionally run a little high. I starting practicing HRM in 2001; subsequently, my blood pressure started lowering into the 90's/50's. I gradually decreased my medication and was completely off of it within 6 months.

I've had lupus for almost 26 years and during that time have had numerous experiences of life threatening illness and hospitalization. I had taken prednisone on and off, but since starting HRM, I have not been on prednisone at all.

Betsy Hart-McMannis, Physical therapist

Dedication

We dedicate this book to all those who are preparing themselves for service to others by energizing their hearts.

Acknowledgments

The authors would like to acknowledge the substantial and critical contribution made by Asatar Bair, of Living Heart Media, for sustained inspiration and editorial assistance, as well as for the cover design, references, and book layout. We are indebted to Howard Glasser, creator of the Nurtured Heart Approach, who described the method of recognizing greatness. We would like to thank Jack Carpenter, CEO of Living Heart Media, for his courageous commitment which made this book possible. We would also like to thank Judith Simpson and Doug Johnson for editing the book.

We are very grateful for the substantial support of Peggy Hitchcock and Douglas Drane.

Contents

List of Tables and Figures

Introduction

From Puran Bair

My father has a few months left to live. Lung cancer has claimed one lung already and his remaining lung is crippled with emphysema. He can hardly talk: his breathing is labored and his voice is clouded, yet he speaks more sweetly than he ever did in his life. In the last two years we've become closer than we ever were before.

Dad's emotional heart has opened. How I wish it had happened decades earlier, for him and everyone that knew him. We all would have benefited from the years we might have had of knowing the man he is becoming now. Now, when I talk with him, he asks about my children. He remembers the details of their lives and has a genuine caring about their progress. He is generous with his time, giving to his visitors the precious little breath he has left. But what touches me most about Dad now is his sweetness and openness. He smiles a lot. He still gets angry when he's afraid or confused, same as always, but now he admits it's his own feelings, which are not the fault of the Catholics, Jews or politicians. He is self-deprecating in a gentle way instead of the self-denigrating way he used to have. He is altogether lovable, and he has more real friends, people who care for him, than he ever had.

The event that changed him was traumatic; it happened four years ago. On their 50th wedding anniversary, my mother was in the hospital, unconscious, in the last stages of a pneumonia she had contracted just a week before, and dad was holding the plastic flowers he had brought to her, the only flowers the hospital would allow him to have in her room.

Dad cried all that day; I had never seen my father cry before. His wife died a few days later. That was the moment of dad's opening, and he cried inconsolably for months. Eventually his grief abated, but the tenderness has stayed.

From our work with Heart Rhythm Practice, the subject of my first book, *Living from the Heart*, Susanna and I have gained an understanding of the process by which a person's heart heals, opens and ministers to others. We see that dad's heart is opening in different dimensions: his accommodation and concern for others is the width of his heart, his vulnerability and tenderness is the depth of his heart, and his generosity is the forward thrust of his heart. We see, too, that there are wounds in his emotional heart that are still healing, and the inner dimension of his heart is still fragile. If he has time left for these further developments, they will erase his fear and allow him to radiate peace into the hearts of those he loves.

I believe everyone's heart is continually trying to develop its richness and make its greatness known. The heart tries to communicate to us its innate wisdom, for which it doesn't have words. What the heart does have is an enormous magnetism by which it can attract people and situations into our lives to teach us what it knows. But people don't like to be taught, and even less to surrender, preferring the way they know to the way they grow.

My prayer has been to be able to consciously assist the progress of my heart's development. I want to develop that sweetness, kindness and generosity my father has finally come to, before my heart needs to resort to grief to get my attention. I want to grow and change quickly enough that I will have time to be of some use to others. I also want my heart's healing so that its creativity and courage can emerge in my life.

This is my work, and I hope this book helps others do the same.

From Susanna Bair

The most remarkable discovery we've made in our decades of teaching is the effect of conscious, rhythmic, full and balanced breath coordinated with the heartbeat. This is the defining characteristic of Heart Rhythm Meditation, HRM.

The conscious breath is the basis of all meditation. Dr. Andrew Weil, the leading proponent of Integrative Medicine, gives the following statement about conscious breath, which is essential to our method of energizing the heart:

The single most effective relaxation technique I know is conscious regulation of breath.

In many languages the words for spirit and breath are one and the same (Sanskrit prana, Hebrew ruach, Greek pneuma, Latin spiritus). Breathing is the bridge between mind and body, the connection between consciousness and unconsciousness, the movement of spirit in matter. Breath is the key to health and wellness, a function we can learn to regulate and develop in order to improve our physical, mental and spiritual well-being.

Breathing is special in several respects: it is the only function you can perform consciously as well as unconsciously, and it can be a completely voluntary act or a completely involuntary act, as it is controlled by two sets of nerves, one belonging to the voluntary nervous system, the other to the involuntary (autonomic) system. Breath is the bridge between these two systems.

Most people do not know how to breathe so as to take full advantage of the nourishing, health-giving properties of the act of breathing. Knowing how to perform simple breathing techniques can help lower your blood pressure, calm a racing heart, or help your digestive system without taking drugs. Breathing has direct connections to emotional states and moods -- observe someone who is angry, afraid or otherwise upset, and you will see a person breathing rapidly, shallowly, noisily and irregularly. You cannot be upset if your breathing is slow, deep, quiet and regular.

You cannot always center yourself emotionally by an act of will, but you can use your voluntary nerves to make your breathing slow, deep, quiet and regular, and the rest will follow.[1]

While some meditation techniques stop at just making the breath conscious, not changing it at all, Heart Rhythm Meditation follows Dr. Weil's advice to set the breath into a deliberate pattern -- full, rhythmic and balanced -- which then sets the heart into the same rhythm. HRM is the only type of meditation that also makes the heartbeat conscious. This is a powerful way to energize the heart, physically, emotionally and spiritually.

Energizing the heart causes a reworking of the memories and impressions the heart holds as wounds. This is very interesting to me as a therapist and a teacher of therapists. I

---

1 www.drweil.com

have seen that working with the dimensions of the heart, in myself and with my clients, gives the ability to control one's mind, in particular with respect to worry, anxiety, fear and low self-esteem. It makes it possible to intervene in the unconscious realms of one's being, which results in a profound emotional and energetic healing.

This is personally very important to me. I had a sister who was mentally ill and I have often wondered how it might have been if my sister could have energized her heart with this method. I wasn't able to help her, but I console myself with the hope that I can help other sisters or brothers of our one family, not only to pull out of mental illness, but to heal energetically their grief from the loss of their mother, father or child, their rejection in love and their guilt and resentments, and come fully to the meaning and purpose of their life.

Energizing your heart goes far beyond healing; it can actually bring forth your greatness, which is far greater than anything you can imagine. What we identify as the "I" is what makes the difference. While people usually identify with their minds, by energizing the heart, the real "I" can be discovered and brought forth. The heart-centered self is much greater and glorious than the mind-centered self. With the heart as the center of identity, the ego is not a problem; it's a resource.

When the Virgin Mary was visited by the angel Gabriel, she exclaimed, "my soul doth magnify the Lord."[2] Ten years of Catholic school have impressed me with a deep respect for the sacred, which I have tried to make real for myself. I think you'll find that energizing your heart leads to the profound experience, "my heart doth magnify my soul."

---

2 Luke 1:46, King James Version of the Bible

In the ten years we've spent helping people to energize their hearts, it's become clear that this is the foundation of a new therapeutic system and a modality for success. This system completes the method of energizing the heart that we started with HRM, taking it beyond meditation, into daily life. As other therapists have come to us to learn these methods, we've all found it not only speeds the process of revelation that occurs slowly in talking therapy, but also provides clients with a tool they can use on their own, to help meet all of life's challenges. Furthermore, it extends therapy far beyond the alleviation of dysfunction to the discovery of the greatness of one's being.

Energizing your heart has proved to be a powerful method to work with both consciousness and energy within the heart; for me, it has been the treasure I sought my whole life. Through meditation on the heart I am able to experience the beauty and power of the soul. Through teaching groups and individuals, I am able to share this treasure with others. I'm so grateful to have the opportunity to share this method with you and I hope the feeling in my heart comes through to yours in these pages.

Background to This Book

The Heart is the Focus

The topic of this book is the heart and the love it contains; we show how to open your heart and fill it with energy. We show how to use the power and tenderness of your heart in many different aspects of life. When we speak of the heart we're referring to a multi-layered center.

- The heart is a physical structure performing an essential function in your body -- not only circulating your blood but creating hormones and beating out a rhythm that informs and regulates every aspect of your body.

- The heart is the center of your energetic system, through which flows the magnetism and light that powers your physical heart and body, gives rise to your emotions, enlightens your mind, and connects to all other heart energies. We call this the energetic-emotional heart.

- The heart is also the core of your self, your inner source, your connection to the Infinite, and the ultimate embodiment of all that you are and all that you become in your life.

We explore the dimensions of the multi-layered heart and develop a language for describing it. Then we present a method of energizing the heart so it can become great -- great in compassion, courage, creativity, vision, cooperation and confidence. All you want in life and all you want to become is a product of your heart.

Physical, energetic-emotional and spiritual -- these are three levels of "heart" that are layered, the latter within the former, and if you give attention to the outer, the inner heart connects with it. Access your physical heart and you'll find energy and emotion. Dive within the inner world of heart energy and emotion and you'll find your spiritual core. The way to the emotional and spiritual heart is through the heart of flesh!

Breath Moves Energy in the Heart

In the work of the heart, we involve and use the body. We work with the body as an instrument of the soul, governed by the heart. Your body is infused with consciousness and energy which create it continually, and your body has an effect on both your consciousness and energy.

When you move energy within your body you can reshape your energetic heart, move emotion, and cause a lasting change in your approach to life. You move energy by the way you breathe, for breath is the essential stream of life. When your breath moves through your chest, it connects your physical body to your energetic and spiritual body; it is the breath that allows you to energize your heart and it is the breath that makes real transformation possible.

You'll see that when your breath touches your heart a wellspring of emotion results that empowers kind, noble, creative and courageous behavior that can truly be called "living from the heart."

A Method with Three Steps

We describe a method of energizing your heart that has three steps:

1. **Recognition:** Recognizing the Dimensions of the Heart in yourself and others.

2. **Meditation:** specifically Heart Rhythm Meditations.

3. **Application:** Activities called "Exercises for Life" that carry the method into everyday life.

This is a beautiful mix of active and passive processes -- at times you'll observe yourself and others and feel the emotion of your heart. At times you'll remember your ideals, aspirations, gratitude and admiration. This inspires your natural creativity and confidence. At other times you're deliberately trying to unfold some of the powers and qualities of your heart that are not often used.

We will present these three steps as if they are done in sequence, but you'll actually do them in concert, as often as you can remember them, as a part of your life that enriches the whole life.

What You'll Find

What will you find when you energize your heart? First, a lot of emotion and energy, some of which might be perceived as pain. Past experiences have been stored in your heart whenever they couldn't be integrated as they occurred, saved for a later time when you would have enough energy and insight to process them. Concentrating on your heart will reveal what has been stored there; then the power of your heart will give you the needed energy and insight to do that inner processing you couldn't do before.

Even if there is discomfort, beneath it is a source of profound happiness, a happiness that needs no reason. Your heart opens more and more as it receives your conscious attention, like a flower that opens one petal at a time. As it opens, you'll benefit from deeper relationships, more meaningful work, greater accomplishments, and improved health.

As you energize your heart you'll find your greatest qualities: lifelong passion, guidance in all things, a compelling vision of your future, compassion, cooperation, confidence and courage. With the power of your heart you will love your life, appreciate your challenges, be optimistic about your difficulties and bring everyone in your life into your embrace. You will experience the integrity of your self; all that you do will demonstrate that integrity.

The next discovery is of your connection to all people, directly, heart-to-heart. Because of this connection you can actually feel in your own heart what another person feels in their heart. This experience may convince you that you have discovered humanity's common resource, the One Heart which all share, and that would be an event of enormous importance. Your discovery of it helps blaze a trail that others may more easily follow.

Then comes the remembrance of a mission, a purpose for your life that was the reason for your birth. This sense of purpose is imprinted into your heart at its creation and when you energize your heart, you find your purpose. To the degree that your purpose becomes your conscious commitment, your heart makes available its reserve of courage and creativity. Your heart has a power that is only available to accomplish your heart's own wish. That power cannot be used for the plans of your mind; all the wonderful qualities of your heart are reserved for, and can be applied to, your unique mission in life.

Safe and Effective Method

As we've developed this method of energizing your heart and seen the changes in ourselves and others who use it, we've witnessed many times that this method is reliable, safe and effective. As you practice these instructions you will indeed feel the effect on your heart. Even without practicing, reading this book will make you familiar with the language and milestones of the process so you will know what your heart is capable of delivering.

To be successful in energizing your heart you'll need a strong method, commitment to a regular practice, a clear underlying theory, and the help of supportive friends and/or a teacher. The practices you'll find in this book will help your determination, and the principles of the heart described here will help you understand your path.

In the path of the heart we do not aspire to the state of consciousness in which there is no personal thought, and beyond that no thought at all; rather, we aspire to an energetic union in which we experience all emotion, and then a spiritual union in which that emotion becomes so much bigger than ourselves that it is truly cosmic. The experience of energizing your heart leads to the ultimate human experience, encapsulated in the mystics' mantra of paradox: "I am a part of all things, and all things are a part of me." This is not an experience of transcendence; it is the experience of the heart enveloped in the Universal Heart which contains all hearts.

Chapter 1

The Heart

1. The Heart

1. The Heart

Where your heart is, there is your treasure also.

--- Jesus Christ

Man's ideal shows the height of his heart.
Man's understanding shows the depth of his heart.
Man's perception shows the length of his heart.
Man's sympathy shows the breadth of his heart.
But the fourth dimension of man's heart is seen
by all that it contains within itself.

--- Hazrat Inayat Khan

The dimensions of the heart's treasure chest
Reveal the measure of character best
Love, joy, courage, creativity
Derive from your heart's activity
Of both body and mind, your heart's the core
Your opened wide heart opens every door.

1. The Heart

The Nature of the Heart

This Chapter

Before we can describe the four dimensions of the heart (Chapter 2), how to measure the four dimensions (Chapter 3), and then how to expand the heart in those dimensions (Chapters 4-8), we need to define what we mean by "heart." This chapter describes the physical structures of the heart center, the way the heart sends out messages to the body and the world, the radiance of the heart as magnetism and light, and the relation of the heart to the mind and soul.

The Homonyms of "Heart"

The heart which is our focus has three general aspects: the physical heart, the energetic-emotional heart, and the spiritual heart.

- The physical heart is visible and material. Its function is to circulate oxygen and dispose of waste gases, trigger the immune system and send a coordinating signal to every cell. It may control a body the rhythm of which is slow and steady, or fast and responsive, or some other rhythm.

- The energetic heart is invisible but measurable and its emotions are observable. Its function is to provide magnetism to the body, to broadcast the heart's state into the outer world, and to receive the energy of the environment and other beings. The energy of the heart may spread out far and wide or be held within; it may run deep to communicate with the essence of all life or rise high as a torch to illuminate new discoveries; it may project forward in power or backward in receptivity.

Whatever direction the heart's energy takes, it creates the corresponding emotions.

• The spiritual heart is invisible and transpersonal. It is evidenced in the qualities of your being, for example, peaceful, graceful, truthful, joyous, creative, intuitive, disciplined, responsible, etc. The qualities of your being direct the energy flows within your heart that results in the rhythm of your heartbeats and the actions of your life. **Being** becomes **doing**. Influence operates in the other direction as well -- doing builds up the qualities of being.

These three hearts are linked so closely that each affects the other; in reality they are entangled as one heart, inseparable.

• When there is a disparity between your personality and the qualities of your spiritual heart, you will despair and your emotional heart can offer no comfort.

• When you have emotional distress, your physical heart will suffer, and this is a very great problem -- throughout the world, cardiovascular disease is the number one cause of death.

• Physical limitations may cause unhappiness.

• The emotions of self-pity can cripple the spirit.

• But confidence in your spiritual connection and a sense of purpose in your life will give you real joy, and optimism can prevent and turn back physical illness.

• A healthy, powerful body is a source of great comfort and gratefulness.

• Caring and kind feelings for others enhances the qualities of the spiritual heart.

The health of each of the three hearts affects the others.

Your Heart Contains Your Treasure

You have a great treasure within you, one that can't ever be taken from you, upon which you can draw continually. This treasure is your heart, and its heartbeat is a constant reminder of its presence. The heart has an extraordinary ability to expand and develop when given attention and energy. The heart has an incredible beauty, gentleness, creativity and confidence, and these qualities are much more abundant in our lives when we are aware of our hearts. Feeling your heartbeat is proof that you have begun to access your heart.

What Protects the Heart Also Hides It

Your joy, creativity and courage are among the extraordinary products of your heart, the greatest assets of your life. But in order to preserve your treasure, you may have encased it in a vault. Effort will be required to find this inner pearl through its insulating layers. You will be continually guided by its throbbing and feeling. Your heart will respond to your effort to access it and become increasingly radiant and sonorous. As your heart receives your attention, it will blossom into your life and all that heart contains will be available to you. Your open heart will open the doors of opportunity in front of you, as every heart opens in response to an open heart. It is the qualities of your heart that make you most attractive to others, and most useful to the world. It is your heart that reveals to you your deepest desires, and gives you the power to successfully achieve them.

At some time in their life, everyone comes to their heart. It may come early; it may come late; it may be embraced as the missing element of life, or it may be rejected. One can live without awareness of the heart, but not well. Energizing your heart is the prerequisite for the great accomplishments of your life.

Your Emotional Heart Is Easily Wounded and Quickly Healed

As you begin to make your energetic-emotional heart conscious, you will find it sore from the wounds of the "slings and arrows"[3] of life. The heart is very sensitive and impressionable, so it is easily hurt. Encountering its wounds may deter you from going farther. But while the emotional heart is easily wounded due to its receptive nature, it is also resilient, and it's capable of rapid healing. It contains its own medicine; it heals itself, when given attention and energy. A method for doing that is presented here and is easily learned, and by this method you can energize the greatness of your heart for its own repair and expansion, and for the benefit of your relationships and work.

The Heart Contains As Much Love As It Can Hold

Everyone has a heart, but the capacity of that heart varies greatly. You can behave with grace and nobility when you have energy in your heart, but when that energy runs out, you can become fearful, stingy, uncaring and mundane. You can recharge your heart, but every expression -- words and deeds -- depletes the heart, some more than others. The heart is also depleted by old hurts that leak energy through open wounds. The capacity of your heart, and the condition of its wounds, determines how long you can hold your heart energy and therefore how quickly you will be depleted by life.

Energizing your heart in daily practice also increases the capacity of your heart to hold more energy. It's like putting

---

3 William Shakespeare, Hamlet (III, *i*, 56-61)

coins in a piggy bank -- when you consistently put in more coins than you take out, you need a bigger and bigger bank.

Consider your heart to be a container of energy. What is the energy that the heart contains? We call this energy "love." We mean by this not some romantic, poetic notion, but a powerful energy that drives your unconscious decisions, draws people and resources to you, inspires your most creative ideas, and gives you the self-confidence and courage to follow them.

The Physical Heart Center

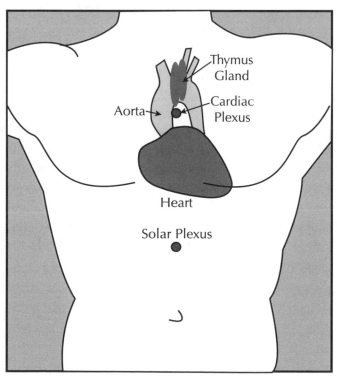

Figure 1: The Physical Heart

Locations of the Physical Structures

We're going to be working with the physical heart and three other physical structures in the center of the chest. When we think about the heart, these four structures all receive attention: (1) the physical heart organ, (2) the solar plexus, (3) the thymus gland and (4) the cardiac plexus. Furthermore, they all receive energy from the breathing practices that focus on the heart, as described in chapters four through eight.

The cardiac plexus and the solar plexus are key points in the nervous system. The thymus gland is part of the endocrine system, responsible for releasing the "T" cells that trigger the immune system. The heart organ is the center of the circulatory system and is also a major hormone-producing gland.

The locations of these structures define an area we refer to as the "Heart Center": the Solar Plexus is the lowest point, defining the bottom of the Heart Center as the point just below the bottom of the ribcage. This is a very sensitive spot, and a very vulnerable one. The cardiac plexus and the Thymus gland are at the mid-point of the Heart Center vertically. They are located just behind the sternum, approximately one rib up from the midpoint of the sternum. The heart organ is slightly to the left side of the circular Heart Center. The top of the sternum defines the top of the Heart Center at the collarbone. (The width of the Heart Center is defined energetically, in the next section.)

Effects of Attention and Energy on the Heart

Attention and energy given to the thymus gland results in an immediate improvement in the immune response. This was demonstrated in 1988 by Dr. David McClelland of Harvard University in a classic experiment in psychoneuroimmunology. He showed a film to 66 Harvard students about

Mother Teresa caring for orphans in Calcutta; an equal number got a film about World War II. Before and after the films he took a saliva swab from each student. Those who watched the film about Mother Teresa showed an increase in the immune system marker in saliva, S-IgA, immunoglobin A. This boost in immune response due to stimulation of the energetic-emotional heart has since been called the "Mother Teresa effect." It was researched again in 1995 by scientists at HeartMath.[4] In our model, the boost your heart receives from exposure to a greater heart energizes the "inner dimension" of your heart and that increases the heart's ability to power your body.

We have found that giving attention and energy to the solar plexus, the bottom of the Heart Center, develops the dimension of heart we call "depth," where the deep emotions become more accessible and useable. This intersection of the depth of the physical heart with the depth of the emotional heart demonstrates how the different aspects of the One Heart are linked.

Attention and energy on the height of the heart, at the collarbone, energizes the heart's ability to communicate its vision and inspire others with its idealism and optimism. These are the qualities we associate with an "elevated heart." These descriptions of the energetic-emotional heart in different dimensions are described in the next chapter.

---

4 Rein, Atkinson et. al. (1995)

Heart Rate

Figure 2: Entrainment of the Breath and Heart Rate

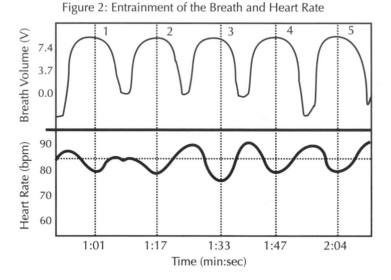

The heart organ is connected through the nervous system directly to other major organs and is able to sense their need. The heart also responds to adrenaline in the blood flowing through it. With these inputs the heart is able to adjust its rate to accommodate the needs of the whole body. By its heartbeat, it is able to broadcast a common signal to every cell.

Thus the heart coordinates the entire organism, and also gives us a model for heart-centered leadership: listen to everyone, and whatever you say, say it to everyone. The heart has no secrets; it includes others and loves to be self-revealing. It's the mind that calculates, "What can I say to whom, for what effect?" The heart knows it absorbs the emotions of many and its own emotions are continually broadcast to all, so secrecy is futile.

Because the heart is continually adjusting its heart rate, the heartbeat is not a constant signal. Internal and external stimuli, including thoughts, emotional reactions, and changes in your environment trigger immediate changes in heart rate so that a beat will come slightly early or late; this creates heart rate variability (HRV), a part of normal cardiac function.[5]

In a non-meditative state, there is no discernible pattern to the heart rate variability. In Heart Rhythm Meditation, the pattern becomes a smooth sinusoidal curve, as seen in Figure 2.[6] Also, the heart rate enters into a state of harmony called entrainment with the breath rate, also shown in Figure 2. Notice the peaks on the top graph (labeled 1 through 5); each one is the top of an inhalation, and it is clear that each peak of the inhalation occurs precisely at the lowest point in heart rate variability, the bottom of the heart rate curve.

As far as we know, this effect hasn't yet been studied; it's certainly not commonly known, even in cardiology. The effects of conscious breath are not much recognized medically at this time.

Figure 2 shows the heart rate pattern is determined entirely by the breath pattern. You cannot control your heart rate directly, but by controlling your breath, which you can do, you cause your heart rate to follow the pattern of your breath. This ability to indirectly control your heart rate is essential to energizing your heart and applying the power of your heart to your life. This effect is so strong, that we've observed that heart arrhythmia disappears during Heart Rhythm Meditation.

---

5 Malik and Camm, eds. (1995), McCraty, R., M. Atkinson, et al. (1995)

6 Our thanks go to Dr. Steve Bauman of the Rhine Institute for conducting the test from which the data in Figure 2 are drawn.

The Heart as a Transmitter

The heart is a kind of transmitter, similar to an FM radio transmitter in that it combines a constant, "carrier" frequency with an information stream. Any electrical current alternating at a constant frequency will broadcast as an electromagnetic transmitter, but it can't carry any information unless some characteristic of that current changes over time. In AM radio, the transmitter varies its amplitude (volume) in time with the music while maintaining a constant frequency. In FM radio, the amplitude is constant but the frequency changes slightly around the constant "carrier" frequency in time with the music. A radio receiver translates the AM change in amplitude or the FM wobble in frequency back into an audio signal.

Like an FM transmitter, your heart produces a variable frequency that conveys a complicated message. If your heart rate was perfectly constant, it would convey no meaning other than a timer; it would sound like a single, steady note. But your heart rate is much more complex, sounding more like an orchestra of many "voices." Those voices convey a great deal of information about your physical and emotional state. Your heartbeat is a centralized, coordinating message broadcast from your heart to every cell. Your heartbeat transmits both the stabilizing drumbeat of a timer and information about your physical and emotional state.

We use an instrument that graphs a person's heart rate over time. By examining the pattern of your heart rate, how it speeds up and slows down over time, you can identify different emotions and dimensions of your heart. Some examples are given in Chapter 3.

A number of remarkable experiments have demonstrated that the HRV of one person can affect another person, through touch, or even through close proximity without touch.[7] It seems that some scientists are beginning to confirm what mystics have known for centuries, that the heart communicates its state to others without words.

Because the heart rate encodes the emotional state, it is literally true that the emotion of the heart is broadcast throughout the physical body as the pulse causes every cell to throb. As the cells pick up the heartbeat they adjust themselves to the current emotional condition. Therefore, emotion is felt everywhere at once: all your cells sing when you're happy, and physical discomfort is widespread when you're emotionally miserable.

The Energetic-Emotional Heart

Table 1: The 7 Energetic Centers (Chakras)

Called	Number	Located
Top of Head; Crown	7	Fontanelle
Center of Head; Third Eye	6	Pineal Gland
Top of the Spine; Throat	5	Atlas
Center of the Heart	4	Cardiac Plexus
Depth of the Heart	3	Solar Plexus
Sexual Center	2	Bottom vertebrae
Bottom of Spine; Root	1	Bottom of Coccyx

---

7 McCraty, R., M. Atkinson, et al. (1996)

The Heart *Chakra* Is the Center of the Energetic System

The heart is an energy center, identified in Yoga as the middle "*chakra*," meaning "energy center" of the seven centers located along the spine and in the head. The heart and the other *chakras* are containers which each store a particular type of energy. The heart is generally recognized to be the leading and controlling center of the whole energy system, as for example in acupuncture.

In Sufism, it's the third center that's called "Qalbiya," the "heart center of subtle energy," while the fourth center is called "Sirriya," the "secret of the heart." This is in keeping with the Sufis emphasis on the depth of the heart, the womb of one's rebirth. In the temple of the body, the *Sirriya* is the altar, the holy of holies, the place where the secret of life is held.

The Hands as the Breadth of the Heart

Sideways, the energy of the heart moves beyond the shoulders to the arms and down to the hands. The palms of the hands are called "secondary *chakras*," extensions of the heart *chakra*, and it is the work of the hands that demonstrates the qualities of the heart. The hands define the "width" of the heart. The one who can embrace a wide segment of humanity, as when the arms are spread wide, and who easily extends a hand to others, is called "broad." The one who keeps his hands to himself is called "narrow."

Hands-on healing is done with the hands, which focus the healing power of the heart. The hands are both sensitive and powerful, like the heart. In an energized heart power is balanced with sensitivity which results in a practical application of the heart's breadth. When we concentrate on the hands, we energize the width of the Heart Center with the result that our influence spreads wider and our lives become more stable.

The Heart Creates a Magnetic Field

There is scientific evidence of the energy center of the heart. The human body has a magnetic field, caused by the electrical currents that move through the nerves and muscles. When the body is still, the center of the magnetic field is the heart organ, which is of course never still. At any given distance away from the heart, the magnetic field has different intensities at different angles -- left, front, right, above and below -- and the pattern of these various intensities shows the dimensions of the heart.

It is significant that the heart is the magnetic center of the body instead of the spine or the brain. The brain does generate a magnetic field as well, since there are always electrical signals in the brain, but the heart's field is a hundred times stronger.[8] A person's magnetic field radiates out of their body into the space around them, combining with the magnetic field of others in proximity. Consequently, it is the heart that is directing the energy transferred from person to person rather than the brain.

Magnetism is literally energy; it converts directly into electricity when it intersects a conductor. Electricity moving in a conductor radiates a magnetic field around the conductor, so electricity and magnetism are interchangeable. In the human body, the heart generates a powerful electrical signal to cause contraction of the heart muscles. This electrical signal flows along the nerves, especially the spine, which acts as its

---

8 Some research on this has been done by Dr. R.H. Kraus, Jr., Biophysics Group, Los Alamos National Laboratory.

antenna. The magnetic field generated by your heart becomes an electrical signal in another person's body when your magnetic field meets the electrical conductor of their spine. This is proven by the fact that one person's heartbeat can be identified in the brain waves and nervous system of others.[9]

"Energy applied over time" is the definition of power, so it is scientifically correct to say that your heart is a biological source of power. A heart doesn't move a compass needle but the human body is very sensitive to magnetism, and the magnetic sensation we have of a person is a key part of our comprehensive assessment of their "presence" or "atmosphere."

The mystics say magnetism isn't created by the body; rather the body is created by a pulsing magnetic field contracting and condensing into matter. According to that view, the heart is the main focus of the energy that generates the body.

The Heart Generates Light

The heart also emits energy as visible light -- all hearts do, and when you energize your heart you can make this bioluminescence stronger, leading to the condition that people recognize as "radiant." This light has been scientifically measured on a photon counter in an experiment that showed 100,000 photons per second coming out of the chest of a Heart Rhythm Meditator.[10] The threshold for visibility is about 1,000 photons per second, so the light of the energized heart is easily visible and creates a lamp in the chest.

The light emitted from the heart is experienced as the color of the sun, yellow, but when the heart is observed from

---

9 McCraty et al (1999)

10 Bair (2007)

above, the top of the Heart Center appears green. (The color green is just above yellow in the light spectrum.) This is why the heart chakra is colored green in the systems of transcendent traditions, but colored yellow or gold in the systems of body-centered mystics.

> *Red at the bottom of the spine, golden yellow in the heart chakra, and blue in the eyes and violet in the third eye, and a white hue very much like a diamond, with all the different colors of the spectrum, in the crown center. The heart center is really the vital center of the aura; it radiates just like a sun. And by concentrating on it intensely, imagining that your heart center is the sun, you will immediately enhance the radiation of your aura.* [11]

It is telling that the common expression for a generous and radiant person is to say he or she has a "heart of gold," rather than a "heart of emerald."

The light of the heart radiates outward in all directions, but it has two main conduits: one is upwards into the brain, causing brilliance in the mind, and the other is forward, radiating from the chest like a miniature sun.

A Stream of Energy Runs Through the Heart

The energy of the heart is experienced as a stream that enters on the left side and emerges on the right side. The stream switches sides in the head so that the right side of the heart powers the left hemisphere of the brain, and vice-versa. From the point-of-view of the heart, it is the energy of the

---

11 Pir Vilayat Inayat Khan, "Practices," contained in "The Leaders' Manual," published by The Sufi Order International.

heart rising into the brain that determines which hemisphere is dominant. If the left side of the heart is stronger, the side where the energy stream enters the heart, then one is more receptive and appreciative of the world, and the right hemisphere of the brain is dominant. If the right side of the heart is stronger, where the energy stream leaves the heart, then one is more expressive and courageous towards the world, and the left hemisphere is dominant.

The left-right balance in the heart changes throughout the day, and there are also longer trends over months and decades. You could be a generally out-going person who is having an unusually sensitive moment, for example.

Normally, people do not experience that they have any control over how the energy in their heart is balanced. You have probably noticed that you are more receptive and reflective around receptive and reflective people, or in quiet, beautiful, or sacred environments, and you become more expressive and courageous around those kinds of people, or in situations that are highly stimulating. So it's clear that the energy balance of the heart can be influenced, but can it be consciously directed?

The Mystical Secret: Breath Directs Energy

The way to direct the energy flows in the heart and to increase the light output and the intensity of the magnetic field is to consciously work with the breath. Energy rides on the breath. By breathing in specific ways, to be described later in this book, you can energize the heart in any dimension.

The Spiritual Heart

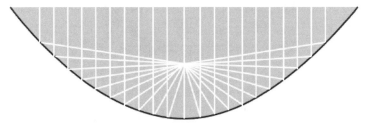

Figure 3: The Heart Reflects the Light of the Soul

Your Heart Is the Focus of Your Soul

Your soul is the highest, most pure, aspect of your individuality; it is likened to a light of a unique blend of frequencies. The ethereal light of your soul shines most brightly in your heart, and is then disbursed throughout your body, manifest in every cell and encoded in your DNA. The mystic views the soul as the force which creates the heart, which then creates the mind, and then the body.

The bottom of the heart acts like a parabolic reflector that focuses the light of your soul on a spot in the center of your heart where it is collected and radiated outward. This is pictured in Figure 3. The bottom of the heart is at the solar plexus, which mystics have referred to as the womb of the soul.

While your soul is the seed of your self, your heart is the focus of your soul. Your heart is the flower that produces a new seed in its fruit-gift to the world.

Consciousness, Vibration, Light, Love, and Peace

Consciousness is the intelligence of the universe contemplating itself. As consciousness develops it concentrates and disburses, and these peaks and valleys create waves, the fundamental vibrations of the universe which power creation. Vibrations clash and the interference patterns create areas of light and dark. This cosmic light is the fabric of existence, which is collected into the light of the soul.

Each soul has a unique blend of frequencies, which are colors, and intensities of those colors. When the light of the soul is collected in the heart, it is transformed by the heart into a special kind of energy called love. When energy in the heart is felt moving, it is experienced as emotion.

As it was formed, your heart was impressed with the wish of your soul, and for your whole life this wish has circulated as a deep current of emotion in your heart, driving and guiding your life. As the heart becomes conscious, this guidance emerges as interests, then intense and creative desire, and then courageous action.

The energy of love flows within your heart, and this motion creates emotion. Some emotions arise from ascending energy flows; some emotions result from descending energy; some emotions flow to the left or right or forward. These motions stretch the heart in the direction they move. When all the energy of the heart is experienced at the same time, this is the emotion of peace. Peace is not passive; it is active, spreading out to reach others and bring them into harmony.

Love may be expressed in many ways, such as creativity, compassion, cooperation and courage. Love creates confidence and a compelling, optimistic vision of the future. Love is inspired by beauty, and beauty is created by love.

The One Heart Reflected in All Hearts

Through your heart you are connected to all beings; there is only one Heart. Each person, animal, plant and stone has a kind of mirror within themselves in which the one Heart is reflected. What appears to be your own heart in your chest is actually a reflection of the only Heart that exists. Thus, every emotion that is felt by anyone is an aspect of the emotion of the one Heart. We each attribute or connect our emotion to different experiences, saying that he makes me laugh, or she makes me happy, or loss makes me sad, or a religious ritual makes me feel exalted, but really those emotions and all emotions are present in every heart all the time.

The Heart and Mind

The Heart as a Lake

The heart and mind can be distinguished, but they are closely linked too. The heart is like a lake and the mind is like its surface. The heart and mind affect each other the way the depth and the surface of the lake interact. The movement of emotion within the heart creates waves of thoughts on the surface, and steady thoughts swept by a persistent wind at the surface of the lake can create a movement within the heart of the lake. This metaphor is also instructive, showing us that the creative impulses of the heart appear suddenly and surprisingly in the mind, which cannot anticipate the inspiring forces of the depth. Furthermore, it takes a pattern of many repeated thoughts on the surface to form an impression in the depth of the heart, which is why frequent repetition is required to learn something "by heart."

The mind changes quickly, like the pattern of wind-driven ripples on the surface of a lake. The heart's direction is enduring, like the powerful current that runs deeply through the lake's depth. It's the steady direction of the heart's desire that gives one a compass in life.

Accessing the Images of the Heart

Your heart is your well of creativity, a container of emotions that give rise to your best insight into the hearts of others, your most beautiful and inspired ideas, and the guidance you need to make holistic, systemic decisions. It can be terribly frustrating to know that you know all this in your depth, and not be able to bring it to the surface of your mind. There is a way to gain access to the images and impressions of your heart, and that is to breathe consciously, which opens the door between the conscious mind and the unconscious mind, the heart.

Breathing is the only activity of the body that can be performed either consciously or unconsciously. All other bodily functions are permanently assigned to either unconscious control, like digestion and heartbeat, or to conscious control, like swallowing and smiling. Breathing can be completely controlled, even to the point of passing out if the breath is stopped too long, or breathing can be ignored and performed automatically. To accomplish this dual control, the breathing mechanism is duplicated: there are two, completely independent sets of muscles, nerves and areas of the brain that can perform breathing. When you breathe consciously, the part of the brain that was performing unconscious breathing is freed up and takes on a new task that is otherwise not normally performed -- it serves as a shuttle to convey information between your conscious and unconscious. Therefore, in meditation you will notice a surge of creativity as images and stored impressions emerge from unconscious levels of your heart onto the screen of your mind.

Connection Through the Heart

In one's heart one feels the interconnection of all people, like water lilies that appear to be separate plants on the surface of the lake but are shoots of one plant underwater. The mind is best at distinguishing differences and perceiving separateness, while the heart loses distinctions in feeling the whole. The mind does analysis (separating something into parts in order to understand it), while the heart does synthesis (combining a thing with its context or environment in order to understand the entirety).

The heart's contribution to life is enriching: it is the source of all the pain and all the joy. The mind observes; the heart experiences. The mind can be above everything; the heart is part of everything.

The Knowledge of the Heart

Only by the heart's knowledge can one become genuine; with the mind alone, one doesn't know enough of one's inner reality to have integrity. The opinions of the mind, however hotly argued and defended, are easily abandoned when the heart is touched. When the beliefs of your mind and heart are different, it can only be due to ignorance of the heart's wisdom. When you know what your heart wishes, it quickly becomes your mind's wish too.

When the mind and heart are disconnected, the mind spouts its own ideas while the heart goes on directing your life, drawing people and situations to you as it needs and causing your unconscious behavior, that is, all the behavior that is not planned, understood or directed by your conscious mind. Then you seem to be two people; one who speaks about going north and one who acts by walking south.

Integrating Heart and Mind

While the mind and heart work in very different ways, they can become aligned and cooperative. Over time, you can develop a reliable access to your heart, allowing your heart to play an increasingly greater role in your life. The heart leads, the mind follows; the heart is the master, the mind is the servant. Then life becomes miraculous as one's plan and one's wish converge and serendipity and discipline conjoin.

The process from discovery of the heart to the establishment of a heart-centered life, the topic of this book, is referred to as "Energizing the Heart." This process occurs in four dimensions.

The Goal of the Heart

Toward Living from the Heart

Energizing the heart is the objective; living from the heart is the goal; this book describes a method for both.

The heart we speak of is physical, energetic-emotional and spiritual, integrated together: a heart that is anchored in your chest as your heart of flesh, that holds the energy of your emotions, and that connects you to all beings. The mystical heart, the poetic heart, and the organ called heart are homonyms wedded through the mind-body connection. Each affects the other, and the mystical aspect of your heart can be discovered through a concentration on the physical aspect of your heart. Even just holding a sustained thought about your heart, as from reading this book, will shift your self-perception toward the holistic and shift your behavior toward both a greater harmony with your world as it is and a greater effectiveness in changing it to be what it can be. The way of the heart starts with concentration on the heartbeat.

The method we'll describe here is both new and authentic, steeped in the tradition of those pioneers who have gone this way before and flavored with the modern knowledge of science and psychology. It is for those who would heal their heart's wounds, find the reality of their inner world, project their heart outward to create their life, and serve the development of the heart of humanity.

Energizing your heart is an extraordinary accomplishment, beyond the lower goals of finding safety and security, forming relationships, and developing expertise in some field. Energizing the heart is like the stage of growth of a plant where it produces fruit in abundance, far beyond its own need to reproduce. The human heart is much more complex than a plant, so the human heart grows in several dimensions, displaying different characteristics and offering different kinds of gifts in each dimension. Knowledge of this multi-dimensional growth will help us recognize our heart, its effect on our life, and the progress we make in our heart's development.

Cultural Encouragement for Developing Your Heart

We intuitively understand much about the highly-prized quality called heart, and our culture has many words to describe it. An energized heart is magnetic instead of reserved; deep instead of shallow; big-hearted and tender-hearted instead of tight and stiff; generous and creative, not afraid of change; warm, not cool; courageously lion-hearted instead of timid; optimistic, never pessimistic. A person with an energized heart is welcomed wherever he or she goes, and creates a feeling in the hearts of others that makes them energized as well.

Whatever else we have accomplished, the condition of our heart is the proof of what we've become. Publisher Malcolm Forbes says, "To measure the man, measure the heart."[12] The dimensions of the heart are a metric for that measurement.

America in particular has a romantic culture, idealizing the search for a perfect mate, rather than learning to live with an assigned mate as in some older cultures. America also has a high divorce rate because the emphasis is on finding someone with a good heart rather than developing a good heart. If the beloved one disappoints or breaks the lover's heart, then the condition is often seen as terminal, rather than a natural occurrence in the affairs of the heart, to be healed and to stand as a testament to the lover's dedication.

Cultural Discouragement for Following Your Heart

Although every culture recognizes, appreciates and rewards the qualities of the heart, many of the platitudes of our culture and the prescriptions of religion and psychology lead one away from the development of a complete and healthy heart.

For example, the advice of people is usually, "Be reasonable," rather than, "Follow your heart." This is because a culture preserves itself by encouraging its members to behave in a predictable way. Reasonable behavior is aligned with the status quo, whereas heart-centered actions are creative and surprising. Fortunately, there is a shift now toward allowing heart-centered actions, since there is no other hope for solving the problems of our time.

---

12 See http://en.wikiquote.org/wiki/Malcolm_Forbes

As another example, we are taught to look upon the aches and pains of our bodies as symptoms of disease instead of signals from our heart. If, by the use of pain-killers, muscle relaxants and antidepressants we diminish our inner sensations, which are conveyed from the depths of our heart to our awareness through our physical bodies, we lose a most important source of guidance. By consciously energizing your heart you may reduce the need for your heart to speak to you through physical pain.

Change Comes from a Change of Heart

Some spiritual teachers admonish us to change our point-of-view and choose a different way of being, as if it were so simple. We live the way we do because of the condition of our hearts. When we are safe in our heart then we can be compassionate towards others. When we have enough energy in our heart, then we can be courageous. When we discover how to energize the creativity of our heart, then we can be creative in finding solutions to the problems of our lives. It's not done with will-power, and making a decision is not enough. Change comes from a change of heart.

Need a Method and a Model

To energize your heart reliably, well within your life-time, you need two things: a method and a model. A method is presented here that can be practiced daily to produce real, direct, personal experience of the heart. When you don't feel able to reach your heart, and even when you have no idea what your heart feels, the method will work to bring you back to your heart. A model of the heart is also presented because experience can be misinterpreted and even denied. Experience is the engine of growth, but interpretation steers experience. We experience that the sun rises in the morning but that experience can lead us to conclude that the sun orbits the earth. The sunrise experience must be re-interpreted as the earth spinning on its axis so we can understand the reality of the solar system.

What Happens When You Energize Your Heart

The consequences of energizing your heart are that:

1. Your life becomes whole as your mind and heart are integrated.

2. Your heart's influence spreads wider as you are able to understand and connect to many more types of people.

3. Change becomes desirable as your heart's capacity to change and grow through all situations of life is increased.

4. Self-defeating tendencies diminish because your life is directed towards the long-term wish discovered in your heart.

5. Relationships become deep and fulfilling as you approach them with the courage and creativity of an energized heart.

6. The purpose of your life is revealed and the power to accomplish it is discovered. Consequently, your dedication to the purpose of your life increases dramatically.

Chapter 2

A Model of the Heart

2. A Model of the Heart

The Whole Heart

This Chapter

In this chapter we present a model of the energetic-emotional heart in four dimensions. A model can be very useful in understanding something complex -- for example a model of the climate system reveals the interaction of cloud cover, surface temperature, and wind. A good model also predicts how the system it describes could change -- for example, if jet trails increase cloud cover, then daytime temperatures will fall, nighttime temperatures will rise and wind will increase. Our model of the heart is also a model of a complex system; the model describes how each dimension of the heart's energy system operates when it's energized, when it's over-energized to distortion, and when it's weak. It describes how one dimension affects the others and how a weakness might be strengthened.

The model presented here is an energetic model. We're referring to the strength of the magnetic field of the heart in four dimensions, not the physical size of the heart. But because all the aspects of heart are strongly linked, the energy field of the heart will have a strong effect on the physical performance of the heart center -- the heart, lungs, thymus gland, and nerve plexus -- and the qualities of the spiritual heart that are available to the personality.

This chapter is vital to developing the skills necessary to operate the heart. It establishes a vocabulary that is used throughout the rest of the book. In Chapter 3, we will describe six ways to measure the heart's dimensions and then three methods to expand the heart and thereby develop the heart's qualities.

This model of the heart describes four dimensions of the heart's growth and leads to the goal of the illuminated heart, fully energized and consciously directed toward the fulfillment of your purpose in life. The exercises presented here will lead you through the growth in each dimension, step-by-step.

One of our goals is to become conscious of our hearts so that we may be conscious of our effect on others, having more of an influence on the world than the world has upon us. In this way, we become the captain of life's ship, rather than its passenger.

The Round Globe of Heart

We have chosen a simple image to serve as a container for the knowledge we've discovered about the heart. Our picture of the heart refers to its energy and the scope of its influence, not its physical size. (See Figure 4)

Figure 4: The Heart (front view)

We start with a picture of the heart that is round like a globe, but protruding forward in one direction and dimpled in the back, opposite the protrusion. The round shape reminds us of the planet, with the message that all the emotion and experience of the whole world of humanity is contained within each heart and that each person's heart is representative of the whole world. This is the meaning of "microcosm," the reality that every part of the whole represents the whole. While usually it seems that our heart is within us, some times it seems that we are within our heart.

Figure 5: The Heart (top view)

When viewed from the top in cross-section, as in Figure 5, the dimpled globe with forward extension looks like the classic shape given to the heart by poets everywhere. The Valentine's shape has a meaning, expressing something that we all feel intuitively about our hearts, suggesting that the heart both gives, as suggested by the point, and receives, as suggested by the dimple.

The shape of the globe of the heart may be shallow or deep, broad or narrow, expansive above or squashed, protruding to the front or flat. Each of the three dimensions represents different qualities of the heart, readily apparent in one's life. There is also a fourth dimension of the heart, represented by its capacity. The globe of the heart contains water, for water symbolizes love. But the heart may be filled or partially filled, or barely filled, and this describes the heart's capacity for emotion of all types. The emotion in the heart is different at different depths, varying from personal joys and pains to concerns that are less personal, but felt even more deeply.

The different shapes of the energy of the heart produce different kinds of personalities, and our description of these personalities may remind you of other personality types you've heard of. For example, a person whose heart is not strong in the forward direction may appear to be introverted, and the opposite energy, strongly forward, may appear extroverted, to use the terms of Carl Jung, for example. But these two systems do not actually compare at all; it's as if one person wanted to cut up a pie by making wedges while another person wanted to cut it into squares. None of the wedge-shaped personalities will match any of the square-shaped personalities; the systems divide up the pie of all personalities in different ways. Jung's system of personality types came from his observation of his patients' attitudes and behaviors, whereas the dimensions of the heart describe the energetic shapes of the heart that develop into personalities.

The Whole Heart

Let us begin with the circular image for the heart that is full and developed equally in all dimensions. It is broad, high and deep. The development of each dimension corresponds to the different qualities the heart possesses, summarized in Figure 6.

Your heart is like a miniature sun inside your chest. It illuminates your life and powers your actions. Its light guides you and its warmth is what people love in you. The sun of your heart is shining constantly to some extent. By learning about the heart and giving it your attention and breath, your heart can expand its power in all directions.

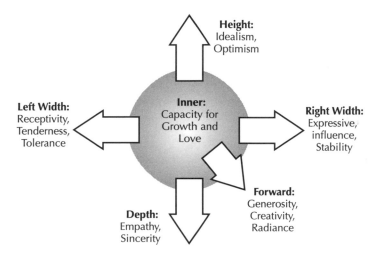

Figure 6: The Whole Heart (front view)

The Width of the Heart

The Broad Heart

The heart can also be broad, extended on the left, the right, or in both directions, making a person "big-hearted."

Figure 7: The Broad Heart (front view)

Characteristics of the Broad Heart

The Broad Heart is like a person with arms stretched wide, welcoming all into an embrace. With a broad heart you are a natural networker who extends your personal boundary to easily include others.

There are two sides to the width of the heart, and one side may be more developed than the other. The left side of your heart is receptive, making you a good listener, cooperative with others, and tolerant. Your easy acceptance makes you well-liked. You don't complain about others and you're not judgmental. You appreciate diversity -- it takes all kinds. What other people do doesn't bother you. Your receptivity quickly picks up the mood of individuals or a group.

The right side of your heart is expressive, making you gregarious, friendly, warm, and influential. You have the ability to harmonize yourself to others and others to yourself. You go out of your way to be helpful to others, even people you don't know.

When both sides of your heart are developed, you easily form alliances with others. You become very stable, like a rock in the stream of life. Towards others this stability becomes loyalty and dependability; personally, it becomes contentment. This contentment makes you inclined to peace and harmony, while less inclined to risk.

The Challenges of the Broad Heart

As a broad-hearted person, you will attract many people who need stability and safety, who want to lean on someone and be cared for, and who recognize these abilities in you. Your stability will be challenged and tested by the many who hang on to you.

Everyone wants the broad-hearted on their side, at their party, to sit at their table. You make others feel more whole and secure, so you are claimed as a friend by everyone. When two groups that don't get along with each other both claim you, it puts you in a dilemma. Unable to alienate or disappoint either group, you'll be pulled in two directions. Also, your accepting nature may be taken advantage of by others who appear to be friendly but are actually exploitative.

The Distortions of the Broad Heart

When your heart is broadened beyond a balanced condition, you may become so accepting as to become permissive of wrong behavior. In your extreme loyalty, you may overlook a serious problem with your friend that can reflect back on yourself. You avoid confrontation, preferring harmony at all costs. You would like to be independent, but you let the group or another speak for you. Still, of all the distortions of the heart, the distortion of the broad heart is the least troublesome.

The Narrow Heart

When the heart lacks breadth, it is narrow, constrained on both sides.

Figure 8: The Narrow Heart (front view)

A narrow heart is isolated. When your heart is narrow you feel intolerant of and inharmonious with others, so you avoid contact, reinforcing your isolation. In the extreme, this creates social phobia where you are extremely uncomfortable among others, especially strangers. With a narrow heart you're uncooperative, unfriendly, easily irritated, misunderstood and intolerant of change. You specialize in a limited, inflexible, narrow range of expertise.

A narrow person is only able to tolerate people who are very similar in background, belief and attitude, and even these people can be irritating at times. People who are different, and most people are, make you uncomfortable, anxious, or even angry. Friendships are rare, but when you have one, you hold onto your friend tightly, even desperately,

With a narrow heart you'll have difficulty working in an organization, even one of your own creation. A narrow heart, if deep, can still be a counselor; if your heart is elevated, you can be inspirational. But a narrow-hearted counselor will soon burn out from overexposure to foreign psychological conditions. If you're narrow-hearted but inspirational, you will likely become cynical because of a lack of public appeal for your specific, narrow ideal. In spite of these limitations, you can still be successful with a narrow heart if you concentrate on your desire.

Nature works to expand a narrow heart through both pleasure and pain. If your heart responds to the love of your friends and family then narrowness is averted and you can become sociable, accommodating and kind, developing into a broad heart. If love fails, then pain may move your narrow heart to reach out to others in search of sympathy.

The aim of nature is to complete itself and as you are a part of nature, your completion is part of nature's plan. If this comes through happiness, that is to be preferred, for your happiness creates harmony. But since with a narrow heart you cannot feel the fullness of happiness, nature may use pain to widen your heart's experience of life. Since your heart is always trying to grow, a useful way to confront the pain of life is to take the attitude that pain comes to you for the purpose of making your heart broad and sensitive.

A gentle and pleasant way to expand a narrow heart is by Heart Rhythm Meditation that gives attention to the heart and uses breath to move that attention sideways. This is described in Chapter 4.

The Depth of the Heart

The Deep Heart

Continuing our discussion of the vertical dimension of our model, the other side is the depth of the heart. The heart with depth emphasizes the emotions that connect all people and the states of being that we have in common. This heart is symbolized by a downward extension to the heart's globe.

Figure 9: The Deep Heart (front view)

Characteristics of the Deep Heart

Your deep heart is empathetic, allowing you to easily feel what other hearts feel as if there was no separation or barrier between you. In the depth we are all united, like water lilies under the water, even though we appear separate on the surface. Because with a deep heart you feel so keenly the reaction of others to your actions, you become very considerate toward others. You are naturally tender and kind. You live in your emotions, so you are familiar with all the feelings that arise, whether desires or fears, longings or anxieties.

Your deep heart is easily moved by the beauty of flowers, the blessing of rain, the smile of a child, or the warmth of a friendly gesture. Scenes in movies and stories of friends affect you strongly.

The depth of your heart will make you emotionally honest. Emotional honesty is different from moral honesty: when a person will not say what is not true, he or she is morally honest, but they may still be hiding their feelings, or be unaware of them. As an emotionally honest person you know what you feel and you're able to express your feelings without distortion. Feelings become your friends; emotions are proof of the energy that moves within your heart.

With your deep heart you are a natural counselor. Because of your sympathetic nature, everyone talks to you and expresses their frustrations and victories.

The deepest emotions are felt here in the depth of the heart, the emotions that are without cause, the emotions that are felt in the heart of humanity. Beneath your feeling of loss, for example, is a much greater sense of loss: the separation of the self from the Source. Loss is experienced at certain times -- at the end of a relationship, pregnancy, job, or the life of a friend -- but the loss of separation is an unconscious, continual emotion in the depth of your heart. Likewise, joy is experienced at certain times -- a new opportunity, the beginning of a relationship, the purchase of a new car -- but there is always a joy in the depth of your heart due to the unconscious, continual discovery of your self reflected in others, in nature and in beautiful things. The deep emotions of separation and reunion are at the heart of your most profound experiences in life.

The Challenges of the Deep Heart

In Handel's *Messiah*, the deep-hearted person is described as, "a man of sorrows, and acquainted with grief." Your challenge is to be able to hold great sorrow -- the price of admission to the heart -- so that you can also feel great joy. Hold open the depth of your heart, from which also rises your deepest sense of happiness and unconditional love.

With access to the hearts of all, it is difficult to separate your own feelings from the feelings of others. In reality, there is no separation between hearts, but people who aren't deep can imagine they are emotionally independent of others -- they don't notice that what others feel they feel also. But you, with your deep heart, can catch the feeling of another person in a glance.

With a deep heart, the awareness of the network that connects all hearts is strong, so you are personally offended when someone acts in a way that harms others. You feel the problems of others as your own, so you take on the struggle of others.

Your deep heart is sympathetic to the pain, confusion and frustration within the hearts of others that can cause them to lash out, and in this sympathy you may even allow them to hurt you. This is incomprehensible to those without depth, but in the depth of your heart you already feel the pain of your tormentors intensely, so the added pain of abuse is not an intolerable increase, and gives a dramatic confirmation of what you feel.

The Distortions of the Deep Heart

When the depth of the heart is increased beyond balance, its extreme sensitivity becomes a distortion. This often causes self-pity and isolation, making the heart shallow and narrow as a self-defense. The inability to escape the pain of others can result in depression. There seems to be no possible relief from the senseless acts of unconscious cruelty that are so common. The solution to this distortion is to learn how to send love from your heart with breath, by breathing out more consciously and fully.

Another kind of distortion of the deep heart is the emotional roller-coaster. To a person without depth, an extreme emotional shift like the change from anger to kindness, for example, is baffling and may appear to be manipulative, whereas the person with a deep heart has access to that fundamental, nameless emotion at the root of all the emotions that can be named. Followed to its depth, every emotion leads to this nameless but very intense emotional base and rises again as a different emotion. The distortion is to ping-pong from one strong emotion to another. Others won't be able to see the connection and will be upset by your rapid change, thinking they're responsible for triggering it. The solution to the roller-coaster is to expand the capacity of your heart (the inner dimension), so you can hold several emotions at once. This will keep all your emotions in balance.

Also, as a deep-hearted person you may suffer from any sense that you are not loved by others. The connection between hearts is so real in your deep heart that you are hurt by any lack of appreciation in others, and especially a lack of appreciation toward yourself. A common lament is, "How could someone to whom I am so connected not appreciate me?"

The Shallow Heart

Figure 10: The Shallow Heart (front view)

If your heart is stunted in the development of its depth, it becomes shallow. This is usually the result of absorbing a powerful emotion from someone in your childhood, an emotion that you couldn't handle. For example, a child's experience of a personal or family trauma, a mother's mental illness, or a father's angry rage can result in a defended, shallow heart. In order to reduce the intensity of your childhood emotional experience, you learned to cut off the depth of your heart where you were the most sensitive.

The avoidance of deep emotion is a very great cost for the relief it may give from a trauma in the past. Emotional distress has a meaning, a cause, and a purpose. If you inhibit any sense of discomfort, you lose part of your inner compass by which you determine what is important and what is not. Pain is a signal that the heart is alive; without it, life becomes mundane. It is through your emotions that you connect to others, so if your heart is shallow you are hard to reach. Shallowness is the condition of a person on tranquilizer drugs; there is no access to the power of the heart's depth. If you avoid depression, you compromise happiness. Your natural condition includes the full range of emotion.

Without access to the depth of your heart, you cannot know yourself. The shallow heart still operates, but largely unconsciously. This causes surprising and difficult events to occur, such as disappointment, tragedy and illness, as the heart and mind move in different, uncoordinated directions. You'll make plans without knowing what you really want.

A person with a shallow heart is usually quite pleasant, but superficial and apathetic toward the plight of others. Those who let their hearts become shallow are uncomfortable with emotion and distrust their heart and the hearts of others. Since they have to rely upon the mind to lead them, their objective is always to be reasonable. Their emotions are as frightening to them as water is to a person who can't swim. Working with the heart will cause some initial pain to those in this condition, but that pain can be borne with the right method, just as one bears the pain of starting to exercise or having a tooth filled.

The Height of the Heart

The Elevated Heart

In some people, the heart is elevated, symbolized by an elongated oval that reaches upward. It is the height of your heart that shows your idealism and optimism.

Figure 11: The Elevated Heart (front view)

Characteristics of the Elevated Heart

An elevated heart recovers quickly from disappointment. This heart has the ability to lift you out of any depression. People with elevated hearts feel joy easily, look on the bright side of every situation, and aspire to the ideal in all matters. It is the height of your heart that lifts your viewpoint beyond the present struggles to see the opportunity being presented to you. It gives you the sense of what is really important, instead of simply urgent. This heart resists getting buried in minutia; it reminds you that you have a higher calling. The honesty of the elevated heart is absolute; honesty is valued for itself, and it is worth maintaining at any cost.

Your elevated heart gives you a confidence that is infectious and empowers others. It inspires excellence and high principles. An elevated heart makes you surprising, humorous, quick, and great to work for -- for those who can appreciate your dynamism. Self-sacrifice comes easily when it's for a cause you believe in.

Challenges of the Elevated Heart

When you have an elevated heart you're difficult to satisfy because you know every situation can be improved. You want wealth, but without any oppression or harm done to anyone. You may shun wealth altogether if it requires compromising your principles. You're hard to manage at work because you're independent and aspire to your own higher goals. Your sense of self-worth is high naturally, so you're not susceptible to the usual motivations of fame and glory.

It is hard for a person with an elevated heart to find a partner; idealists are rare. Anyway, the elevated heart is so capable that working alone is preferable to working with anyone who would lower the standards.

Generally, having ideals makes life more difficult. It's easier to go along with things if you don't care if they're right. Ideals are constraints, even though they are self-imposed.

Distortions of the Elevated Heart

When the height of the heart is increased beyond balance, then the elevated heart becomes excessive and distorted. One distortion is to become critical and impatient with people who resist change, have low standards or not much skill. The opposite distortion is to see extraordinary abilities in others who then disappoint. Another distortion is to be so single-minded in your ideal as to be intolerant of other ideals. For example, being pro-life is a position that represents a high ideal, but the freedom of a woman to choose pregnancy or not is also an ideal. To hold the teachings of scripture as sacred is an ideal, and so is having forgiveness and respect toward those who do not. Idealists may choose principles over people, as for example the king in the play Camelot, who prosecuted his own queen.

The distorted, elevated heart becomes isolated. No one can live up to your ideal, so you becomes cynical. You can't live up to your own ideal either, so you may become self-destructive. If this frustration is managed, it becomes satire instead of cynicism; many comedians have elevated hearts. The height of the heart is distorted, however, as long as one focuses on showing others what's wrong instead of how it could be improved.

Your heart can become so elevated that it loses sight of the ground. Then you become unrealistic. But what is reality if not the reflection of the way we see things? The Wright Brothers were called "dreamers" before their plane flew. Even if you fail, your failure may turn out to be a success in a different way; a breakdown may lead to a breakthrough. But your idealism is distorted if it causes you to miss the steps along the way. You need to keep one eye on the goal in the sky and another on the path on the ground.

The Crushed Heart

Your heart has height naturally, but your heart may be crushed by severe disappointment, intolerable oppression, or betrayal by someone you idealized. When crushed, your heart cannot feel idealism and enthusiasm; it is left without optimism.

Figure 12: The Crushed Heart (front view)

The crushed heart is slow to recover from disappointment. The long-term holds no hope for you if your heart is crushed, so you become short-sighted. Your ideal has been long compromised away so you no longer even aspire to improvement. Cynicism abounds and makes both the present and future miserable.

When your heart is crushed you're hard to motivate. Your trust of others is gone. Your sense of direction and morality can be crushed too. You might justify lying and other unethical behavior as revenge toward those whom you feel have crushed you. In this condition, honesty is seen as a tactical approach, to be followed if it gives an advantage and abandoned if it doesn't. You don't care enough about others to honor them with honesty, and your apathy will even make you numb toward the pain of self-deception.

While this is a common condition of the heart, it is a treatable illness, not a natural human condition. A crushed heart is a kind of weakness within the heart. Heart Rhythm Meditation can restore the natural state of awe, wonder, hope and optimism that makes your life worth living. Recognizing the greatness of others can give you hope and inspiration when you realize that all you admire in others is a reflection of your ideal self. Given the right conditions and encouragement, your crushed heart can rise again and cynicism can be replaced by optimism.

The Forward Dimension

The Driving Heart

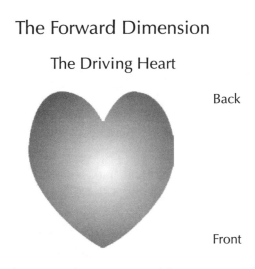

Back

Front

Figure 13: The Forward Dimension of the Heart (top view)

From the top, the heart shows a shape that is used everywhere to symbolize the heart. The classic heart shape comes from our experience that there is an asymmetry about the heart. The heart in its fullest development is symmetrical left and right, but the back is different from the front. In the back, between the shoulder blades, one feels a vulnerability that is symbolized by an indentation. It is here that we feel the betrayal of being stabbed in the back and it is here that we receive the help of a strong hand pushing and guiding us forward. Mystics have long described this point in the upper back as a place where energy flows in, while energy flows out through the front of the heart. One experiences more thrust forward than backward.

Characteristics of the Driving Heart

When the heart extends forward, it sends its power into life, to accomplish the heart's desires and express the heart's emotion. As you come toward such a person you can feel their heart extending forward to meet you. The driving heart is powerful, unstoppable, courageous, charismatic, generous, magnanimous, a natural leader. This heart is like a sun, shining its light into the world. Its power empowers others. When you are in the presence of the driving heart you feel you can do anything, and you certainly can do much more than you're used to.

The driving heart takes the contentment of the broad heart and expresses it in self-confidence. It takes the idealism of the elevated heart and applies it in a practical way. It takes the compassion of the deep heart and turns it into a creative act. All that is in your heart is projected outward, forward, along the direction of your desire.

The Challenges of the Driving Heart

The driving heart can accomplish whatever it desires, so the challenge is not to overload it with tasks but choose carefully what is most important.

While excellent for short-term goals, the driving heart can get off track on a long project. The key is to break up a project into a series of short goals.

This kind of person needs alliances with others who can sense the environment, plan, build networks, and navigate around obstacles while tracking the distant goal.

2. A Model of the Heart

The Distortions of the Driving Heart

If the power of your forward driving heart is increased beyond balance, the "bull in the china shop" syndrome can be a problem -- not being considerate of the effects of your actions on all concerned. You may become destructive instead of constructive.

With a driving heart you feel a rush when you make things happen, and the power and speed of your life can become addictive. You can confuse high-speed activity with progress, intensity with importance. Furthermore, you might think everyone should be able to do what you do, so you are not tolerant of those whose hearts have different qualities. You set an extreme pace and can become impatient with those who can't keep up or who question whether the effort is appropriate.

If you don't find something worthwhile on which to focus the forward power of your heart, you might become paralyzed or, worse, self-destructive. The driving heart has to be applied or it becomes dangerous to yourself and others.

The Blocked Heart

While the forward dimension of the heart is natural, something may happen that stifles that direction. A punishing defeat, especially one that can't be comprehended, results in a blocked heart that is impressed with fear and becomes overly cautious.

Figure 14: The Blocked Heart (top view)

The heart that is blocked becomes unaware of its inherent power and feels it has nothing to do. This is not humility; it is weakness. When the heart is blocked it cannot express itself or satisfy its desires. The human heart contains the greatest power on earth; it can potentially operate the universe to create the conditions and experiences it needs, but when blocked, the energy of the heart cannot project into the world.

A blocked heart will cause you to retreat from the engagement of life. You may be among others and busy with tasks all day long, and still be in retreat. Unable to share yourself, help others, or take initiative with the things you feel strongly about, you can become frustrated and complain bitterly. When you're not successful, you blame your failures on circumstances and others. The very tendency to blame and criticize is a sign of a blocked heart.

Your blocked heart can usually be energized to its natural forward direction by concentrating on something you love, in a supportive environment. Every heart has a strong desire; find it, and the forward power of the heart will return. The desire may begin with a very personal and selfish wish -- no matter. Your desire will progress to become generous and grand as the forward dimension of your heart develops.

The blocked heart can also be helped by feeling a hand on the back of your heart, like the expression "a pat on the back." There is a point in the back of your heart that receives energy; this is symbolized by the indentation at the top of the classic image of a heart. (To correspond to your energy pattern, the image should be laid flat and turned around so the indentation is at your back.) A person's hand, especially their right hand, carries the energy of their heart; when their hand is placed on your back, you receive their heart energy directly into your heart. This can also be done in words of praise and respect. Those who receive praise feel empowered to extend their hearts forward. This is why our method of recognizing a person's greatness is so important.

The Inner Dimension

The Full Heart

These pictures have described three dimensions of the heart: (1) the height and depth, (2) the width left and right, and (3) the front and back. There is a fourth, inner dimension, to represent all that the heart contains within itself.

Characteristics of the Full Heart

The full heart becomes radiant, glowing from within. It creates a quiet self-confidence and sense of freedom. With a full heart, you are always at home, harmonized with your surroundings and the people you're with, in touch with your emotions, desires, and the life-long wish of your heart. Silence is your friend; being alone is always welcome; nature is natural and nature is everywhere you are. Wherever you go, you are aware of representing a great principle, or a great person.

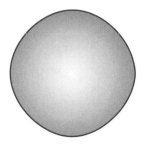

Figure 15: The Full Heart (front view)

A full heart can respond inwardly to any situation, moving easily into happiness, humility, sacredness or peace, regardless of circumstance. Any kind of change is easy, internally or externally. Your emotional state is perhaps not visible externally, but you make no effort to protect yourself; you have nothing to hide and your heart is transparent. With a full heart, you are likely to smile, or at least have a pleasant expression, but unlikely to laugh. Your displeasure might show in a glance, but not a word. You feel no need to blame anyone for anything.

If only the inner dimension is developed, without the outer three dimensions, the heart lacks practice in doing these things. This is the condition of a child, in whose innocence and purity one can see the potential power and beauty that a human heart can become, but who has not yet developed these qualities in their character.

The Challenges of the Full Heart

Your full heart is so flexible and comfortable with change that you may appear to be different at different times, hard to read and mysterious. With a full heart you feel all sides of any issue and consequently you are removed from all arguments and silent on most causes. No one knows where you stand because you stand with all.

It's important for the full-hearted to try to communicate clearly with coworkers and friends so they don't misread you as duplicitous or insincere.

The Distortions of the Full Heart

Your full heart is so complete, you may not feel any motivation to act, socialize, or express yourself, being perfectly content. You will be easily overlooked and underestimated by others, who see no outer evidence of your inner greatness. The propensity to inaction in a very full heart is a distortion. The challenge of life is to develop your inner potentials into one of the outer dimensions of the heart, apply those dimensions, and then energize the hearts of others. The distortion is to feel complete in your potential instead of finding completeness in the fulfillment of your purpose.

The full heart can also become sanctimonious in a kind of fake pseudo-spirituality. If your attention has been primarily within, upon yourself, you might be over-emphasizing inner purity like insisting on a harmless diet, allowing only positive thoughts, or following a dogmatically-correct behavior. That would be a lack of compromise and adaptability that inhibits your full heart's natural freedom and responsiveness.

The Hollow Heart

The heart that is lacking in the inner dimension is referred to as "hollow."

Figure 16: The Hollow Heart (front view)

A heart that lacks fullness is easily exhausted by the demands upon it. After interacting with others, making a small personal change, or performing a simple act of generosity, this heart has to retreat to recharge. If your heart is hollow you are drawn to solitude and nature, avoiding conflict and responsibility as much as possible. The personality created by a hollow heart appears to be complete, well functioning, perhaps even beautiful, but it cannot hold that appearance for long when under stress. This heart can flip from being elevated, deep, broad and forward to being crushed, shallow, narrow and blocked. Therefore the hollow-hearted seek to avoid all stress and tend to resist any change.

Every heart has a limit of how much it can feel, or give. If it goes beyond that limit it must then retract into itself. This limit is the heart's "capacity." Even people who are very good at giving to others, such as health-care workers, can exhaust their capacity in "compassion fatigue." This can happen in any kind of business: sales people get exhausted by making cold calls, operators get exhausted by handling complaints, teachers get exhausted by their students' problems, everyone gets exhausted by the stress of deadlines and the demands of those above. Exhaustion can be countered by inspiration, in other words, by practice in breathing consciously into the heart, as we do in Heart Rhythm Meditation.

The hollow heart can be restored to fullness if it is open and sincere. When the heart is hollow it is in an unnatural condition, just as narrow, shallow, blocked and crushed are unnatural conditions for the heart. Fortunately, the heart is the most responsive faculty in a person. It is easily wounded but can be quickly healed.

The Energized Heart

Putting all these dimensions together in balance results in an energized heart that is elevated, deep, broad, forward and full. The overall shape of the heart is round, like a sun, but indented in the back and protruding forward in the front. We have found this image useful as a metaphor to describe and develop the heart qualities that are needed for a person to reach their full potential as a human being: to give all they have with joy, and to receive all they are given with gratitude; to love without fear or reservation; to know happiness, peace, and fulfillment that are deeper than the transitory conditions of life.

The Heart of an Organization

This model of the human heart can also be used to understand organizations, such as companies, firms, institutions and associations of all kinds. We believe it is useful to see an organization as having a heart, just as people do. The heart of an organization is initially formed by some or all of the founders; later it is manifested in a small group of people within or closely involved with the organization.

A person is a part of the heart of an organization if the condition of his or her own heart creates a similar condition throughout the organization. A change in the organization's heart is immediately expressed in every aspect of the organization, just as the heartbeat is felt in every cell of the body. The head of the organization is the top of the hierarchical leadership, but the heart of the organization can include employees who are not among the top levels of the hierarchy and even some key individuals outside the organization, like the spouse of an executive. The people forming the head have the authority to make decisions, but the people in the heart are responsible for the atmosphere of the organization and are actually more influential long-term.

If one could rule an organization by fiat, giving commands that would be carried out exactly as intended, the heart of an organization could be ignored; only the head would be needed. But even the army doesn't work by fiat. Consideration must be given to the people who form the organization and to the atmosphere that makes it possible for them to contribute best. The heart of the organization is what will make it excel and succeed.

The model we've sketched is, of course, a sort of idealized portrait. While there may be few organizations who exhibit the ideal of any dimension of the heart, we think it is a useful device for understanding the types of organizations and a way of assessing which organizational qualities are more developed and which ones need attention.

The Elevated Heart

The height of an organization's heart shows its sense of excellence. Some companies are humble in their approach, but the company that shows the quality of the elevated heart is convinced it has a much better idea or product than anyone else. This company is committed to excellence above all, whether it's required by the marketplace or not. It has only one kind of product: the best that can be made. Its employees are fanatic, idealistic missionaries. The customer base may be small, but they're enthusiastic!

Within an organization, a person with an elevated heart can put the good of the organization or one of its customers ahead of their own benefit. But those with crushed hearts only focus on their survival through what they feel as demoralizing oppression wielded by the organization upon themselves. They are not motivated by stock options or such future rewards, but can be energized by recognition in the present.

A company shows signs of a crushed heart when the work has lost its joy and the product its excellence. Even companies that were once dynamic and inspired, showing the height of the heart, can become oppressive, fearful, or mundane if the hearts of its leaders are crushed.

A company with a crushed heart may practice deception of its employees, stockholders, the government, or other parties because the pessimists in charge will not see a long-term value in the short-term cost of honesty. Such a company may follow the letter of the law, but only because of the fear of getting caught. Those who feel fooled by life and who have had their dreams crushed have no trouble deceiving others.

A crushed organization can recover if the people at its heart become re-energized. Otherwise, it will suffer from many problems: the best employees will leave because working there is no longer fun or because their own ideals are compromised; customers will be disappointed when the company no longer believes in the high standards it once held, and the company will engage in persistently poor strategic planning because only the height of the heart gives the perspective to see the future.

The Deep Heart

The depth of the heart of an organization is shown by its commitment to service, both in taking care of its employees when they have extraordinary need, and in getting deeply involved with its customers. Some vendors deliver their product and move on, but deep organizations want to get intimately, even irreplaceably, connected to their customers. Instead of staying at arms-length, they embrace their users. A deep company has appeal for those who like to actually help or serve the customers, beyond meeting their immediate or stated need.

Those with deep hearts are connected through strong personal relationships to every aspect of whatever organization they join, hence the deep-hearted know the condition of the organization better than any external analyst, and perhaps better than many within the organization's management. Count on them to represent the customers, the employees and the investors. They don't play games, bait others or criticize; they are incredibly sincere. Everyone likes to work with them, and they attract business like magnets.

On the other hand, a shallow heart may limit one to jobs that are highly repetitive, routine or technical, where the risk of the emotions of challenge and disappointment are limited. Those with shallow hearts can't lead effectively because they can't appreciate the risks taken and the pain felt by others. If one can't be self-revealing one won't be trusted. Even though the shallow-hearted may have the desire to help others, they'll be unaware of their needs, unable to relate to their plight, and uncomfortable around them.

An organization displays shallowness when it does not care what problems its users have, when it acts as though its employees are replaceable and interchangeable units, when it fails to value its relationships with other organizations, and when it measures its success in numerical terms, rather than human terms. The numbers may report the past but the people of the organization form its future.

The Broad Heart

In business, the broad heart is highly valued. The broad hearted person is a mentor and coach to many, and values the ability to succeed through others. Breadth of heart allows a person to be the most flexible, loyal and reliable worker.

The width of an organization's heart determines the scope of its reach, its embrace of diversity and its cross-cultural appeal. This applies to both the organization itself and its communications such as public relations and marketing. The ability of the firm to foster teamwork within the company is the same heart quality that builds alliances with other companies. Its loyalty to its employees goes along with its loyalty to its customers because if the heart of the organization has loyalty, a characteristic of the width dimension, it shows loyalty in all its dealings. The broad heart expands easily, accepting differences and modifying its products and services to suit a wide market. At home, it is accepting of differences within itself. A wide organization welcomes a diversity of backgrounds and opinions.

In a narrow company, the employees have to be like peas in a pod; the customers too. The leadership of the company will be all from the same school, without ethnic or cultural diversity. Since difference is not respected, it is not trusted. Homogeneity of opinion, behavior and appearance is required.

The Driving Heart

In business, the forward-hearted is the one who overachieves the goals that others set by aspiring to his or her own much more ambitious goals. You can see their enthusiasm in their step: they walk like they have somewhere to go. Those with elevated hearts have a spring in their step, the broad hearted have a sure-footed stability, but those with forward hearts have a powerful and purposeful stride.

The forward dimension of the organization's heart shows its ability to be bold and innovative. Some organizations are very cautious in a changing marketplace, but a forward-hearted organization is able to take a step ahead of the others in its industry or field. This kind of organization is forceful and powerful. It will succeed in reaching its goals. It's very exciting to be a part of, if one can stand the pace and pressure. As a participant with a driving heart, your excitement comes from what you accomplish personally, regardless of whether it's worthwhile or meets the customer's needs. The challenge of leadership, then, is to align people's individual goals with the organization's goals.

The organization with a blocked heart is unable to accomplish its objectives, even though it may be elevated, deep and broad. This is seen when activity is high internally, but not directed toward the world outside. Memos spin around, meetings are intense, reorganizations are frequent, but nothing is visible externally. It's like a car on blocks that prevent the wheels from touching the ground: everything runs, but the car doesn't go forward.

The Full Heart

In business, the full hearted are able to redefine themselves, moving from one area to another with such ease that those they worked with realize they hadn't begun to know them. The computer scientist, for example, might surprise everyone with his marketing speech. The head of Human Resources might come up with a new technology idea. Every full-hearted person is capable of internalizing the entire organization.

The inner dimension of the organization's heart shows its capacity to adapt and transform itself. It's not the ability to be bold and take risks (the forward dimension), or the ability to grow its market share (the width dimension). The inward dimension contains the resources the company will have to draw upon as its market changes. This company may change its industry to follow the interests of its customers or the opportunity it sees being unfilled by others. It may transform from an assembler to a manufacturer, or from a Political Action Committee to a research lab. This organization will surprise people with its adaptability and capacity to become whatever is needed. People who work within this organization need full hearts so they are very secure and self-reliant, not dependent on rankings or positions, with a wide range of abilities and interests.

The hollow-hearted organization may be successful at present, but it is still fragile. Some of the largest companies with the greatest market share are actually vulnerable because they depend upon conditions remaining exactly as they are, whereas change is inevitable. This dependency may not be apparent, but it can sometimes be sensed in the assumptions of their business model.

Every organization is limited by the capacity of its heart more than the talent or knowledge of its people. Specialization is linear; creativity is circular. Experience is stabilizing; innovation is surprising. A product, like buggy whips, may be essential for a long time, then suddenly disappear. The full-hearted company doesn't just shift, it leaps to a new definition of itself.

Chapter 3

Working with the
Heart's Dimensions

3. Working with the Heart's Dimensions

This Chapter

In the preceding chapter, we presented a visual model of the four dimensions of the heart; this model is abstract yet described as physical dimensions, based on energy yet expressed as personal traits. These parallels show the linkage between the physical, energetic-emotional and spiritual aspects of the heart.

Just by reading about the dimensions, you already have a sense of the strengths, distortions and weaknesses of your heart. Your response to a description of each is the first way to measure the dimensions of your heart. Another five measurements are described in this chapter. Understanding or experiencing the methods of measurement is not necessary if you already know how you want to energize your heart but if you don't know, then measurement can be helpful. To ensure that your efforts are compatible with your heart's natural growth, a decision-sequence given here will help you recognize which direction of which dimension to energize now.

This chapter also addresses the question, "how does one energize the heart?" The Six Basic Powers are the only resources one can completely control; those powers are described and used in the three methods of energizing the heart: (1) recognition, (2) meditation and (3) application.

The following chapters show how to apply the three methods to each dimension of the heart.

Measuring the Dimensions

Measuring the Magnetic Field

The Magnetic Field Has a Shape

Three of the dimensions of the heart are measurable by instruments that can sense the magnetic field or the visible light that the heart emits. Without instruments, the dimensions of the heart can also be observed by those trained in feeling the magnetic field with their hands, which is objective in the sense that it can be verified consistently by different people trained in this method.

In measuring the magnetic field, we find it is not a uniform sphere surrounding the heart. Rather it has a shape that can differ left-right, forward-backward and above-below, depending on the development of each of the dimensions of the heart that we have described.

The width of the heart may be measured at a distance from the shoulders: the left side of the heart is shown in the strength of the magnetic field to the left of the left shoulder, and the right side of the heart is shown in the strength of the magnetic field to the right of the right shoulder. The width of the heart is also shown in the intensity of the magnetic field around the left and right hands.

The height of the heart creates a strong magnetic field in the front, at the level of the collarbone, and the depth of the heart creates a strong magnetic field in the front at the level of the solar plexus. The forward dimension of the heart can be felt in the magnetic field directly in front of the chest.

Sensing the Magnetic Field by Hand

The technique for sensing the magnetic field by hand relies upon the incredibly sensitive nature of the hands during meditation. Once conscious, full, rhythmic and balanced breath is attained, your hands can be prepared by the following process:

1. Lightly stroke one palm running the fingertips of your other hand from the palm, forward to the fingertips. Brushing over the palm and fingers this way brings attention and magnetism to the hand. Repeat with both hands.

2. Gently blow over one palm, from the heel of the hand forward to the fingertips. Repeat on the other hand.

3. Open your eyes and look at your hands. There is a subtle energy in your eyes that pours out to them.

4. Close your eyes and try to notice three sensations in your hands: (a) a throbbing throughout your hands, echoing your heartbeat, (b) a feeling of pressure in your palm that changes with your breath cycle, going in your palm as you breathe in and out of your palm as you breathe out, and (c) a constant tingling sense like an electric field around your hands, neither throbbing with the heartbeat nor changing with the breath. You might get one of these sensations now, but with practice you'll feel them all.

5. When you are aware of all three sensations in your hands, they are ready for use as incredibly sensitive instruments. Test this by turning the palms of your hands toward each other, as if you were holding a large rubber ball between them. Bring your hands closer together, never touching, by pushing through the magnetic field

repulsion. Then pull your hands apart and bring them toward each other again, as if you were playing an accordion. Look for levels of magnetic force between your hands that resist as your hands move closer. These are the layers of the magnetic field of the heart, expressed through your hands.

6.   Now you can apply one of your energized hands to sensing the magnetic field of another person. Look for a layer of energy that surrounds the person's body. Your hand can run along this layer, feeling its dips and swells in different areas.

7.   Notice the distance from the body to this magnetic layer as you pass your hand over the front and to the sides of the shoulders. The absolute numbers aren't meaningful, as it depends as much on the sensitivity of your hands as on the intensity of the other's magnetic field. But the relative numbers show a shape that reveals the heart's dimensions.

Observing Patterns of Heart Rate Variability

One of the instruments we use often in teaching about the heart is a computerized calculator of Heart Rate Variability (HRV). It picks up the heartbeat of a person by an infrared sensor on a finger or earlobe. Then it measures the fractions of a second between heartbeats. Dividing that measurement into 60, it calculates the number of heart beats per minute (bpm) there would be at that rate and graphs that point on a time scale. When the next heartbeat comes, either slightly sooner or later than predicted, the heart rate is recalculated and graphed again. The time between heartbeats doesn't stay constant -- the graph shows a heart rate that can jump very quickly or rise and fall smoothly.[13]

We have noticed several correlations between the HRV pattern of the physical heart and the dimensions of the energetic-emotional heart:

1. Excursions of the pattern above the average heart rate show the height of the heart.

2. Excursions of the pattern below the average heart rate show the depth of the heart.

3. The length of a rhythmic wave shows the breadth of the heart.

4. A rhythmic, stable pattern following an unstable pattern shows the forward dimension of the heart. The amplitude shows the power of the driving heart. If the pattern can be held through questioning, it shows persistence.

Elevated Heart Rate Variability

Figure 17: Heart Rate Variability

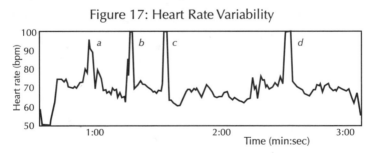

Figure 17 shows a graph of the heartbeat of a subject who was not meditating and who experienced four periods of mild emotional distress (labeled *a*, *b*, *c*, and *d*) when he was

---

13 Malik and Camm, eds. (1995) offer the first medical textbook on this topic in their book *Heart Rate Variability*.

asked about his finances. His emotional distress caused a momentary spike in his heart rate each time. His heart responded to the "emergency," speeding his heart rate to around 100 bpm to increase blood flow so the muscles and nerves would have all the energy they would need for quick action, then fell back to the resting rate of about 70 bpm as the thought passed. The stress this caused on his heart is similar to the stress on a car that accelerates very fast from 70 mph to 100 mph, then decelerates just as fast.

Between these stressful moments there is a jagged graph that shows no evidence of a rhythm. The lack of rhythm in this person's heart rate will also be expressed in a lack of rhythm in his life. He has very little breadth or forward dimension to his heart, and that will show in a lack of stability and drive in his affairs. The forward dimension of his heart is not strong enough to drive away his fears, hence the reaction of distress.

Figure 17 shows the heart rate rising quickly without descents, a characteristic of an elevated heart. (The dips at the very beginning and end of this graph are due to the instrument.) Such a heart responds to challenges by leaping, not slumping.

Elevated, Deep and Driving Heart Rate Variability

Figure 18: The Effect of Heart Rhythm Meditation
on Heart Rate Variability

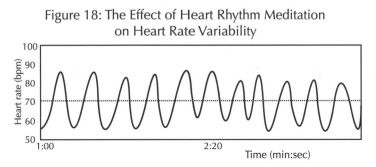

Time (min:sec)

Figure 18 shows the same person a few minutes later, practicing Heart Rhythm Meditation. He is breathing in and out every eight heartbeats, or one complete breath cycle in about 13 seconds, at an average heartrate of 70 bpm. Thus the heartrate is following a pattern that is completely set by the breath rate, cycling through smooth peaks and valleys, falling and rising as the breath comes in and out. This shows how conscious, rhythmic breathing creates a rhythm in the circulation system that can then be felt in every cell of the body, through the pulse.

The practical value of this is that the subject was asked about his finances repeatedly through the meditation time this graph covers, and the previously stressful subject did not affect his heart rate at all. This shows a very powerful and useful way of responding to stress, not by avoiding or denying it, nor by fighting it in reactive combat, but by expanding the ability of your heart to handle stress. Stress is unavoidable because it is nature's way of stimulating growth, and growth is what is required of us all. But what is stressful to a weak heart is not stressful to an energized heart. Instead of fight or flight, meet your stressful challenges and appreciate their function. The ability to hold a smooth breath pattern through stress shows the power of the driving heart.

In an organization, rhythm is also vitally important. There must be periods of expansion and contraction, production and research, enthusiasm and constraint, buying and selling. Sensing and controlling this rhythm is the chief activity of the management.

When the pattern of heart rate shows high and deep waves, as this graph does, the height and depth dimension of the heart is well developed. The smooth waves show an *amplitude*, or change from peak to trough, of more than 30 bpm, far beyond the typical value of 10 bpm. This shows that his heart is able to respond to his breath. When we see that, we know his heart is also able to respond to his emotions, as he responds to the emotions of others and affects their emotions with his own.

Apparently the depth of his heart has become energized by Heart Rhythm Meditation, but we know from the first graph that the depth of his heart is not usually available to him outside of meditation. Therefore we recognize in him an elevated and driving heart, but not a deep heart.

If we hadn't seen his heart rate variability without meditation, we would say this is an ideal graph, a visual picture of an elevated and deep heart (large amplitude), that is driving forward (no change during questioning).

Deep Heart Rate Variability

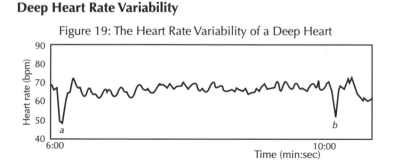

Figure 19: The Heart Rate Variability of a Deep Heart

Sometimes the heart rate will show sudden descents, indicating a slowing of the heartbeat. Figure 19 depicts the HRV of a subject who is not meditating; the graph shows two moments when the subject's heart dropped more than 10 bpm (labeled *a* and *b*), and no moments of rising heart rate. We have found this correlates to a person with a deep dimension to their emotional heart. Such a heart responds to challenges by slowing, while the emotions go deeper.

Shallow Heart Rate Variability

When the HRV pattern is flat, as in Figure 20, it shows little change in heart rate over time; this means the heart is behaving mechanically, like it does on a pacemaker. When the pattern is flat, the heart is too.

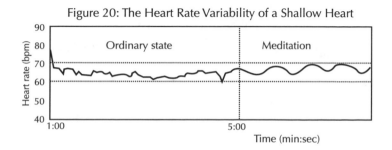

Figure 20: The Heart Rate Variability of a Shallow Heart

Figure 20 is a picture of a shallow heart that does not respond to the signals from the other organs of the body or to the breath, and is unmoved by the height of others' joys or the depth of their suffering. The subject for this graph is new to Heart Rhythm Meditation; notice that during meditation long, rolling waves appear in the graph, but there is no increase in amplitude, which remains about 10 bpm. Without amplitude, his heart has very little power. He will likely show the characteristics of a shallow heart, especially isolation. This can be changed if the height and depth dimension of the heart is energized.

Broad Heart Rate Variability

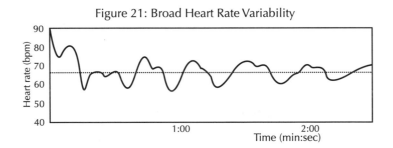

Figure 21: Broad Heart Rate Variability

Figure 21 shows the HRV of a person who is not meditating; there is a regular rhythm to this rounded pattern, which shows emotional stability. This pattern would not be so remarkable during meditation, but to have this without meditation shows the peacefulness of a broad heart. This person was asked questions while sitting with us, but the heart rate showed no sudden changes throughout. The broad heart can just absorb difficulty, handling gracefully what others could not and maintaining a regular rhythm.

Narrow Heart Rate Variability

Figure 22: Narrow Heart Rate Variability

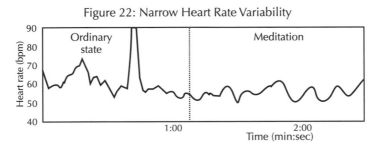

If the pattern is irregular and jagged, as in Figure 22 to the left of the dashed line, it shows some kind of discomfort or anxiety -- this heart lacks width and is not stable. Something that is not wide can be easily tipped to one side or another. The rate of change in the heart rate and the amount of change from the base heart rate correlate to the intensity of the anxiety. The abrupt peak in heart rate occurred when she was asked about something in her life that was very disturbing for her. Notice that she was able to create a broad pattern during Heart Rhythm Meditation. With practice, that smoothness will persist even when she is not meditating because the breadth of her heart is energized.

Blocked Heart Rate Variability

Figure 23: Blocked Heart Rate Variability

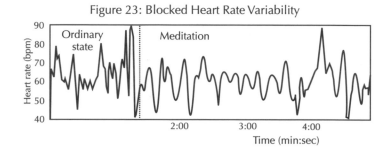

The heart rate pattern can also show determination and perseverance, qualities that show the forward dimension of the heart. In most people, the heart rate pattern changes when they are disturbed by voices or other sounds, but in a person who has a strong breath, which gives determination, the pattern of breath dominates the heart rate regardless of the environment. This power was shown in Figure 18. Practically all Heart Rhythm Meditators can control their breath when practicing alone, without distractions; the ability to do it while people are talking demonstrates mastery of one's emotional space.

In Figure 23, the subject was not able to maintain a smooth pattern during meditation. This shows a lack of concentration and an inability to control his breath. If he could have controlled his breath, he could have made his heart follow the smooth pattern of his breath rate. If he can't concentrate enough to make his breath rhythmic and stable, his lack of concentration will lead to failure at other things too. His blocked heart is not transmitting a consistent, powerful wave, so his influence will be slight, but still much better during Heart Rhythm Meditation than not.

Assessment by Questionnaire

The dimensions of the heart can also be determined through a computer-scored questionnaire called the "Heart Index" located on the Internet at:

http://www.heart-rhythm.org/emotional/index.shtml

Here are some sample statements from the Heart Index, that you assert or deny by degree. One question may affect several dimensions, some positively and some negatively, so the scoring is complex, best done by a computer. We encourage you to go online and respond to these statements. You'll receive a four-dimensional score showing the current shape and capacity of your heart.

- There is something that happened to me 10 years ago that I still resent.

- When talking with people, I don't like to reveal what I'm feeling.

- I have a quiet time everyday in nature or my backyard.

- I've found something I can do that will reliably pull me out of depression, without drugs.

- I feel an inner longing in my heart that can't be satisfied by external things.

- In a team project, I gravitate toward the most difficult task.

- In my family or group of friends, I bring the ones who are drifting away back into the group.

- I try to avoid emotional pain, even if it means avoiding others.

- When I'm working on something, I can get lost in it.

- When I promise to do something, I follow through, even if I no longer want to do it.
- With me, what you see is what you get. I'm pretty transparent.
- I suffer personally when my friends suffer.
- I go for periods of a month without speaking to my parents (or relatives, if parents are deceased).
- There are no heroes in life.
- I feel grateful to have the parents I have.
- I have anxiety and fear about becoming sick.
- I find myself getting into arguments about politics.
- I take a pill at the first sign of a physical pain.
- I don't have time for meditation.
- I find my first impressions of people are generally right.
- When what I want doesn't happen, I remain hopeful.
- I try to see the best in people.
- The ignorance of those who don't know what I know is my advantage.
- There are times when it would be foolish to tell the truth.
- I find most people are very different from me.
- When a friend is talking to me about their problems, I take their point-of-view so completely that I can't argue with them at all.
- There are some perfectly legal ways of making money that I would never do.

Since filling out a questionnaire relies on a person's subjective answers to questions, it lacks the external verification of direct observation, but we have found that the magnetic field measurements, the Heart Rate Variability pattern and the Heart Index correlate very closely to form an assessment of the relative strengths of the height, depth, width, and forward dimensions of the heart. The inner dimension is assessed by only the Heart Index.

You may think that scientific measurement, questionnaires, and assessments in general are incompatible with spirituality, which is often concerned with matters of the unseen world, requiring faith in that which cannot be perceived. To the contrary, we emphasize measurement and verification because the risk of imagination and projection is high on the spiritual path. We are describing a method which has many levels of feedback so you can objectively gauge your own progress without dependency on another's judgment.

The Dimension of Your Pressing Need

Everyone has some pressing need. Consider, what is being asked of you right now in facing the challenges of your life and responding to the needs of those you serve? Your pressing need is the stimulus for your growth. Whatever problem or challenge you face now, it will require some growth of your heart in one of its dimensions. If no growth was necessary, it would not still be a pressing matter; you would have already resolved it. What dimension of your heart will your pressing need require? Whereas the other assessments show the present dimensions of your heart, your pressing need shows what dimension of the heart is trying to emerge in you.

By meeting your pressing need, you will energize that dimension that its solution requires.

Assessment by Breath

You can assess the relative strengths of the dimensions of your heart by a special breathing practice which directs your breath into the heart's four dimensions. This practice works because you already have an experience of the size of your energetic heart. From an observation point in the center of your heart, you can literally feel the distance to the edge of the heart in each direction. The instructions are as follows:

1. Sit up straight with your shoulders back. Close your eyes.

2. Be aware of your breath flowing in and out of your nose.

3. Think of your heart. When you succeed at placing your attention on your heart, your heart will respond with its heartbeat. Feeling your heartbeat is proof your attention is in the right place. If you can't feel your heartbeat, then press your index finger and thumb together -- with the right amount of pressure, you can feel a pulse in your fingertips. Or press your fingers into the center of your chest to bring out the heartbeat in the chest or the pulse in your fingers.

4. Imagine that you are inside your heart, like a large room in which you are central.

5. As you breathe out, imagine your breath reaches from your position in the center of your heart to your left, as far as it can go until it's stopped by the wall of your heart in that direction. Do this for at least five breaths, and notice the distance that your breath seems to reach before it is blocked.

3. Working with the Heart's Dimensions

6. Repeat in the right direction.

7. Send your breath upwards to the height of the heart, until your breath reaches the roof of your heart. Do this for at least five breaths, and notice the distance that your breath seems to reach before it is blocked.

8. Repeat in the downward direction, sending your breath to the bottom of your heart.

9. Breathe forward and let your breath reach as far as it can until it is stopped by the forward wall of your heart. As before, repeat for at least five breaths and notice the distance.

10. Finally, breathe out deeply, breathe in deeply and hold your breath. Feel the size of the heart that your breath fills.

This breathing practice gives you a sense of the relative size of the dimensions of your heart. The actual distances are not significant; it's the relative distances that are important. Which distance was the greatest? Did you feel your heart was wider to the left or right? Did it extend further upward or downward?

This is your direct experience of your heart as it is now. This shape can change in a matter of months as you energize your heart, and the impact of that on your personality, relationships and lifestyle will follow immediately.

Using the Six Basic Powers

The next three chapters will describe three steps to energize the power of your heart. These three steps all use basic
abilities that everyone possesses, although they are seldom
used consciously. We call these human abilities the Six Basic
Powers, and you use them wherever you are -- at your desk, or
dinner table; in a meeting, car, bed, or prison cell; while walking, standing, sitting or talking. No one can take these powers
away from you, but you might be unaware of how they affect
you and everything around you.

The Six Basic Powers are your **intention**, placement of
attention, **inspiration** and expiration of breath, physical posture **position**, self-produced **sensation**, and a sixth basic
power that people rarely use: **invocation**, as in prayer. These
are the only powers you have and the only powers you need.
By the combination of these basic powers, you have learned,
performed and become all that you have learned, done and
are. These are the powers you will use further to energize your
heart.

Intention

The universe is designed to respond to you; you are the
active agent, and the infinite resources of the universe are at
your disposal. You program the universe by holding a specific
intention. The more specific and whole-hearted your intention
is, the more quickly the universe will arrange itself to assist
you in its accomplishment. If your intention is not fulfilled, the
first thing to consider is whether some part of you was uncomfortable with your intention, or whether you changed your
intention before it could be delivered.

The universe acts like a huge wish fulfillment system; you place your order, and then the universe delivers, after some delivery time. The lag between order and fulfillment is built-in to the system so that insincere orders are self-canceling. If you cancel your order during the delivery time and order something else, the precious resources of the universe are not wasted on something you no longer want. So you must hold your intention steady until the order is delivered, and very few people do this.

In energizing the heart, we will start with a clear intention that results in an observable change. The dimensions of the heart give us the language to make our intention clear. It is not enough to say, "I want to be a better husband (or wife)." Your intention must be more specific so you know how to focus your process of change and clearly see results. You could say, for example, "I want to be more accepting." That would specify a particular quality in the width of the heart. Then, since acceptance is difficult to conceive of abstractly, it is helpful to apply the quality to a particular situation. So you could say, for example, "I want to be accepting of my wife's perfectionism." Now you can track your progress in that specific kind of acceptance and know that acceptance is also growing in your heart in general as the width of your heart expands.

Knowing you are working on the width dimension of your heart, you could also track the change in your ability to listen to your spouse and others, your stability and contentment under stress, and your effectiveness in creating harmony and teamwork among others. Depending on which dimension of your heart you wish to develop, your attention will be placed in a specific place in your body, on specific sensations, and on certain observations in your interactions with others.

Having the intention to change is not enough to cause change. How wonderful we would all be if we could simply choose to be different. We are the way we are, with the heart qualities we have and the problems that accompany such hearts, for good reason. The desire to change is certainly necessary, but it is not sufficient. To create change, your desire must be consciously declared as a specific intention, and then the intention must be carried out by a method appropriate to that intention.

Attention

It is commonly said that change requires vision and energy. Vision is really two powers: intention and attention. Part of what is meant by vision is a clear end-goal, which is part of one's intention, while another part of vision is paying attention to the process. Whatever you measure will change; whatever you notice will be affected by your attention. If you want to lose weight, for example, your intention would specify how much weight, or how you would look when you attain your goal. Then your attention would have to be placed on the measurement of these factors to observe the change, and on the aspects of your process, such as what you eat and how you exercise.

Your ability to place your attention is an innate ability -- no person or circumstance can take it from you. Getting your attention is the main activity of both your friends and enemies. Advertising is the business of getting attention, and you are surrounded by stimuli that demand you see or hear, and then think of, a message from some advertiser. Even your body demands attention and, if necessary, uses pain to get it. In spite of these demands, you can always choose where you direct your attention, and this choice determines your life.

3. Working with the Heart's Dimensions

When you choose to place your attention on your heart, a miracle occurs -- your heart, basking in your attention, opens up and begins to speak, lead, and empower your life. If you want to live from your heart, you have to be aware of your heart -- your heart must receive frequent and strong doses of your attention.

You will be using attention both internally and externally. That is, you will place your attention on your heart and notice internal sensations that will guide you through your process of energizing your heart. You will also direct your attention to the hearts of others and notice the various dimensions of their hearts. By these acts of conscious attention you will be transported to a beautiful world of beautiful and highly energized people, and you will feel the same qualities within yourself.

Inspiration (Expiration)

Energy is also required to achieve a goal. Energy is usually confused with "motivation." In losing weight, for example, motivation is important, but "energy" is still different. Your **motivation** determines the strength of your **intention**; motivation keeps your intention before you and creates persistence in that intention. The **energy** you apply to weight loss is seen in your breath; breath is a stream of energy. When you're losing weight, you're breathing differently than you were when you were gaining weight, and that shows the different energy you're applying.

Since we realize that energy comes from breath, we call the accumulation of energy, "inspiration," and the application of that energy, "expiration."

The use of energy in fueling transformation is a feature of the path of the heart. The heart cannot be energized "in cold blood;" it has to be warmed by breath. The flames of love are fanned by gentle blowing. In Heart Rhythm Meditation we breathe into and from the heart.

Mystical poetry often refers to the need to warm, or even melt, the heart.

> Love can always be discerned in the thought, speech, and action of the lover, for in his every expression there is a charm which shows as a beauty, tenderness and delicacy. A heart burning in love's fire has a tendency to melt every heart with which it comes in contact. [14]

Whereas the image of cold or freezing is never used to express the heart ideal.

> Warmth melts, while cold freezes. Drops of water falling on a warm place and on a cold place are affected differently. The drop in the warm place spreads and becomes larger, covers a larger space, whereas a drop in the cold place freezes and becomes limited. [15]

Again, the warmth which melts the heart comes from the action of breath upon the heart. It is essential that we know how to breathe to create this effect. A shallow breath won't do; it has no passion. A fast breath won't do either; it blows out the fire. To do the job you need a long and complete breath that is directed into and out of your heart.

---

14 www.hazrat-inayat-khan.org: Message: Complete Works: Volume 5, Love, Human and Divine: The Philosophy of Love.

15 www.hazrat-inayat-khan.org: Message: Complete Works: Volume 5, Pearls from the Ocean Unseen: Blessed are They that Mourn.

Position

By sitting in a noble position your heart becomes noble, and a noble heart makes a person noble. So we use a noble posture for Heart Rhythm Meditation: the sitting position of the pharaohs. It may be counter-intuitive, but when you're feeling low energy, try sitting up, chest forward, shoulders back, spine straight and head level. Taking that position rather than lying back will give you strength as your heart energy revitalizes your whole body.

The four-legged creatures have their hearts toward the earth; only the two-legged mammals have their hearts directed forward as they meet each other. Does this give humans an advantage? We think so -- since the heart is both a sensitive receiver and a powerful transmitter, the direct heart-to-heart position must facilitate a transference of energy and information between people.

The tendency to round the shoulders, round the back and slouch has the effect of partially hiding the heart. This can be a defensive posture. Men, especially, have the tendency to stand at an angle when speaking to each other, not directly across from each other but a little sideways. This shows an insecurity; it is bold to stand directly opposite another.

You often get the advice that you should "face your problems." Perhaps the real meaning of this is that you should position your heart so that it directly faces the person that challenges you.

Sensation

You will perceive sensations in your body when you think of your heart, but more important are the sensations you create. There are two kinds of sensations: those produced by emotion and those produced directly by attention, perhaps also with pressure. The path of the heart is not a dry path; it is full of emotion. You need to approach your heart humbly, with the emotion of reverence, and you will be rewarded with the emotions of joy, bliss, grief, longing -- all the emotions, culminating in peace. It's all love in its various flavors, for love is all the heart does. Whenever you have emotion you have many sensations that the emotion causes in the body.

You can create sensations by attention, with and without pressure. The first sensation to look for in Heart Rhythm Meditation is the pulse, which can be felt anywhere in the body. You might feel it in your fingertips, in your head, in your kneecaps, anywhere at all. This sensation will be helpful to you because it gives you the sense of your heart's rhythm. If this sensation doesn't occur spontaneously, you can create it by pressing your thumb and index finger together with the right pressure.

The next sensation to look for is the heartbeat in the chest. You can stimulate this sensation by placing your hand over your chest and pressing your fingertips on the sternum, the area between your ribs in the center of your chest. You can also stimulate the sensation of the heartbeat by holding your inhalation. Those who have become proficient in Heart Rhythm Meditation report that by their breath and attention they can create a sensation of pressure in the chest, like the heart is expanding inside the ribcage.

In some traditions a meditator is taught to press the tongue against the roof of the mouth. This creates an upward sensation and a stimulation of the pineal gland that helps lift consciousness upwards and out of the body into transcendence. This is another example of creating a sensation in meditation. We don't recommend it; the path of the heart is a path in life, in the body, in the heart. For this path, you want to stimulate the sensations of the heart.

Invocation

Invocation is calling upon a being by name. It usually refers to the beginning of a prayer, such as "Our Father" (Christian), "Barukh atah Adonai" (Jewish), "Bismillaah ar-Rahman ar-Raheem" (Islamic), or "O Self!" If you have a religious faith, we encourage you to call upon it as you approach your heart, for the heart is the center of all religious worship, and the deep feelings you have for your religion will help you find your heart.

If you don't have a religious belief, and even if you do, we encourage you to call upon your heart as the sacred temple within. Imagine that you stand outside of your heart, requesting entrance. Since your heart is within you, you don't really need to ask, but this device of invoking your heart can be helpful. Typically, you are not in your heart, but in your mind. You wish to descend into your heart in order to energize your heart and find your connection to the divine within yourself and all. So this is a special use of the concept of invocation: your mind is invoking your heart.

Imagine that the Divine Father and Mother, the Lord of the Universe, the Divine Mercy and Compassion or the True Self is within your heart. When you call, it is that spirit within your heart that answers. All you wish for is found in the heart; your heart answers your every call.

Choose a Dimension to Energize

Your "Growing Edge"

Now is the time to consider which dimension of the heart to develop. The heart doesn't grow in all dimensions at once; it has a "growing edge" in one of the dimensions at a time and it's this growing edge that you'll want to energize. You want to cooperate with the direction that growth has already taken. In choosing which dimension to energize, here are a few principles to consider, in priority order.

1. The dimension of heart required by your pressing need is the one to energize, if you can identify which dimension that is. Life is designed to bring out the qualities of your heart by requiring you to grow to meet your challenges. So the dimension of your heart that is being challenged and demanded in your life now is most likely your growing edge.

2. Remember the description of the dimensions of the heart in Chapter 2. If you feel that one of the dimensions of your heart is distorted, then do **not** energize that dimension. More energy in that dimension won't help you; the dimension needs to be complemented with another dimension.

3. Consider the measurement of your magnetic field strength in the different directions, the analysis of your heart rate pattern, the result of the Heart Index questionnaire and your assessment by breath. Did those measurements reveal a very strong dimension? If so, then that is **not** the dimension to energize. Be thankful for the energy already present in your heart.

4. Consider the people you admire; which dimension of their heart do you recognize? Our admiration of others is a sign of what we feel we could possibly become. The more you see in others, the more you can find in yourself. You are attracted to the hearts of others because you recognize the same potential in your own heart. What appeals to you about other people changes over time, as your own growing edge changes. At any point, what you see in others is the same as what is emerging in yourself. Energize that.

5. Did you identify with any of the descriptions of a weak dimension, like the crushed, shallow, narrow, blocked or hollow heart? If so, then choose that dimension to energize. This principle is last because there are typically many dimensions of your heart that are weak compared to that dimension that is most energized right now. One strength makes every other aspect of the heart appear weak. If the first four principles above did not result in a choice of the one dimension to energize, then pick one of the dimensions that is relatively weak.

The Three Methods

We have three ways of energizing the heart, and they reinforce each other so powerfully that their effect multiplies. Each of these three methods use the six basic powers in a different way. The first method is to recognize the dimensions of the heart in everyone you meet, all the time. The second method is to discover in yourself the dimensions of the heart you have seen in others. The third method is to apply the dimensions of the heart to your life, for trying to use these qualities will call them forth and strengthen them. We recommend that you use all three methods together.

Recognizing the Dimensions of the Heart

The first step in energizing your heart is to recognize the aspects of heart in others. The model of the four dimensions makes it easier to see the many qualities that appear in each different heart.

Recognize the Hearts of Friends, Then Strangers

And since you know you cannot see yourself so well as by reflection, I, your glass, will modestly discover to yourself that of yourself which you yet know not of.
-- William Shakespeare[16]

The intention for this first method is to recognize the dimensions of the heart in others. What you see in others you can then find in yourself. If you can't recognize in a friend the qualities of a broad heart, for example, you'll not be able to notice it in yourself either. But when you do see a broad heart operating in a living person, you'll have a clue to finding this same dimension in yourself.

You perform this method largely by attention, inspiration and invocation. Position and sensation aren't required. To become sensitive to the hearts of others, emphasize your inhalation -- literally breathe in the hearts of people around you. You can do this anytime, anywhere -- in the line at the supermarket, in a business meeting, during a conversation, anywhere. To remind yourself that you're looking for the greatest qualities of the human heart, invoke the greatness of the other person. Whenever you say, "great," you're invoking the source of all being, which resides in the heart, and you're tuning

---

16 William Shakespeare, *Julius Cæsar*, Act I. Scene II.

yourself to the great qualities of the four dimensions of the heart.

When you see a deep heart in someone, appreciate it. When you see an elevated heart, praise it. When you see a broad heart, associate with it. When a forward heart appears, acknowledge its courage and creativity. When you find a full heart, stand in awe and wonder before it.

Compliment the Hearts You See

Having recognized the greatness of a person's heart, celebrate it by a compliment. By complimenting others, you strengthen those same qualities in yourself. Compliments echo. You'll receive back and store up all the compliments you give away.

The way you express your compliment describes what you see in the other person. There are three points to remember when giving compliments: first, be completely positive and leave out any implied putdown. Second, state the observable evidence that supports the compliment, and third, connect the compliment to the person's heart, to make it clear you're talking about the person, not their job or behavior.

For a first example, you could say, (1) "You look great," but don't stop there. Add the evidence: "There's a sparkle in your eyes." And then connect it to the inner qualities of the person: "That shows me the height of your heart." Now you're speaking from your heart, about the heart, to the heart of your friend.

Here are four other examples of compliments that incorporate all three points, starting with a completely positive statement, adding evidence, and connecting to the dimensions of the heart:

(2) "I love to work with you; you make people feel they can succeed, because of your consistent optimism."

(3) "You can count on me, anytime. I've seen how you defend other people. I feel a strong loyalty in your heart."

(4) "You excel at whatever you take on, like that last project you did better than anyone I know could do it. You succeed because of your high standards and commitment to success."

(5) "I trust your leadership. I think that decision you just made was hard but it was right. You're very clear and have a lot of integrity."

How Not to Compliment

Don't say the following kinds of things because they contain an implied putdown, don't give evidence, and don't connect to the person's heart:

(1) You're looking so much better. (You looked pretty bad before.)

(2) You're a lot of fun to work with when you're not mad. (You're mad a lot and you're difficult to work with.)

(3) I'll stand with you against the rest. (You've got a lot of enemies.)

(4) You do that kind of task quite well. (You're only good at some specific things.)

(5) I trust you as long as you follow the rules. (I'm afraid you won't.)

Your Heart Has a Great Influence on Others

One of the great discoveries about the heart is realizing how great your influence is upon others, and their influence upon you. Your energized heart can energize the hearts of others, and your closed heart can close the heart of others. Your breath through your heart can disclose the love there and spread it outward, which in turn brings out qualities in the hearts of others. To increase your positive influence, beware of the three things that can close your heart or indicate it's already closed, and cause the same effect in others: criticism, pessimism and indifference.

- **Criticism** is seeing something in another that you don't like. It comes from not seeing deeply enough. When you have insight, you see the beauty and nobility in the hearts of people, even if you have to see through a dark covering of protection. People get very little benefit from being criticized; usually they just become defensive. You can find fault with everyone, and where is the fault? In the mind of the one who finds it. Worse than the criticism is the effect on your own heart of holding a critical view: it closes your heart.

- **Pessimism** is a disease of the heart, a kind of exhaustion that comes on when the heart's energy has leaked out. It causes a negative interpretation of the present and removes your hope for the future. When you speak from pessimism you're speaking from a weak heart and consequently you're incapable at that time of inspiring another. What you think or say about your friend may seem to be true, but it doesn't account for the power and creativity of your friend's heart, which you can't feel when you're in a pessimistic state.

- **Indifference** is a disconnection between you and your friend. If you don't care what happens to your friend, then don't bother him or her with your opinion. Dialogue is valuable -- it's based on a sense of common experience and interdependence -- but there's no dialogue with indifference. The indifferent heart is withdrawn, unaware of the connection between all hearts. Such a heart is shallow and narrow, incapable of communicating from heart to heart. It causes the other's heart to feel abandoned.

Seek and you will find. Tune your sight to the hearts of others and you will be rewarded by visions of the great qualities of the heart's dimensions. What you see you will become.

Meditation

Our second method for opening and energizing the heart is the method of meditating with entrainment of heart-beat and breath called Heart Rhythm Meditation. It allows you to find and experience in yourself all the dimensions of your heart that you have seen in others. You will be using all six basic powers in Heart Rhythm Meditation. Your intention to develop your heart can be fulfilled by sitting in a majestic position, giving attention to your heart, using simple breathing techniques that give inspiration, attending to and developing emotion and sensation in your body, and calling upon the unseen resources of your heart for help.

There are different aspects of Heart Rhythm Meditation that will be employed for the different dimensions:

Table 2: Development of the Dimensions of the Heart

Chapter	Dimension	Developed by
4	Width	Widening Breath
5	Depth	Downward Breath
6	Height	Rising Breath
7	Forward	Streaming Breath
8	Inner	Expanding Breath

The width of the heart (Chapter 4) can be developed by the **Widening Breath**,[17] which coordinates the breath and the heartbeat by becoming aware of both sensations. The resulting stability of this coordination makes the heart wide, tolerant and influential. In practicing the Widening Breath, you will see how rarely one uses the basic rhythm of life where the

---

17 Bair (1998), Chapter 5, The Rhythmic Breath.

intake and the outflow are balanced and how powerful it is when you do.

The depth of the heart (Chapter 5) can be developed by the **Downward Breath** in which you experience a downward flow of energy coming into and pouring out of your heart.[18] The practice is quickly soothing and relaxing, and with practice creates a deep feeling of well-being.

The height of the heart (Chapter 6) can be developed by the **Rising Breath**[19] which increases your inhalation, which is literally "inspiration." To do that, you need to breathe out more fully. You have to expire (breathe out) in order to inspire (breathe in). Developing a full breath is essential for developing your heart, and the first dimension to benefit is its height. The natural buoyancy of the in-breath restores your optimism, high principles and aspiration to excellence.

To develop the forward dimension of the heart (Chapter 7), we will practice breathing forward from the heart, sending breath and its energy directly into the world. This is an amazing experience with a surprisingly strong sensation. You can actually feel a stream of energy and light coming directly out of your chest in the **Streaming Breath**.[20] The result is an increase in the power of the heart to attract what it wishes to attract and move forward in the direction it wishes to advance.

The inner dimension of the heart (Chapter 8) can be developed by retaining the inhalation in a special four-part

---

18 *ibid*, Chapter 12.

19 *ibid*, Chapter 6.

20 *ibid*, Chapter 9.

rhythm we call the **Expanding Breath**.[21] As the breath is held in the heart, the heart is forced to expand. The result is that you will be more "spirited." You will have an inner capacity you can draw upon to transform yourself. The analogy to breath is direct: you will actually expand your breathing capacity and your rib cage as your heart capacity increases. In medical terminology, the volume of air you breathe is called your "Vital Capacity," a particularly apt term.

All of these versions of Heart Rhythm Meditation have certain techniques in common: they all use a full breath, timed to a conscious heartbeat, directed through the heart. This is described in the next chapter in the Widening Breath. From that common base, the six basic powers are tuned differently to achieve the different effects on the dimensions of the heart.

The aspects of Heart Rhythm Meditation described in this book are from the first level of the path that produces the ultimate goal of an illuminated heart. There are three more levels, but this first level is the most important, for here you will find the excitement of the heart's discovery that can give you the determination to proceed toward the goal.

Application

Our third method is a series of **Exercises for Life** that we try to use during the day, all the time. These challenging exercises fascinate and delight us; the slightest success at one of them gives a great sense of joy. These exercises follow on the meditations, bringing them into application in a practical way.

---

21 *ibid*, chapter 8. Also called the Square Breath.

They use the basic power of intention, and direct our attention in different ways.

Each of the following chapters on a dimension of the heart includes a set of eight Exercises for Life to develop that dimension. Once you decide which dimension of your heart you wish to energize, try one of the Exercises for Life for that dimension. You might try one for a few days or weeks, then another, or you might find an opportunity to use several. They will change the way you work and relate to people, making everyday chores and business into spiritual practices that energize your heart and the hearts of others.

Each Exercise for Life is illustrated by a story taken from our lives and the lives of people we've known. To protect the privacy of those that we've observed, we've changed the names and certain other details.

Chapter 4

Stretching the Heart

4. Stretching the Heart

Figure 24: Stretching the Heart

This Chapter

Here we present a meditation, called the Widening Breath, and eight Exercises for Life that stretch your heart in the horizontal dimension, giving you a broad heart. The other dimensions of the heart are addressed in later chapters.

Your Heart May Have Become Narrow

It may be that your heart has become too narrow. This could occur because of a betrayal or loss of a love relationship that makes your expanding heart retreat in the width dimension. You would feel this narrowness as a loss of the social quality you used to enjoy. Your trust in others would be damaged and you would begin to withdraw from your friends and loved ones or at least become very guarded.

Or it could be that your heart was wounded very early by others, reinforced through isolation in your childhood, and established as a pattern of solitude in your adulthood. Such a heart has never known the pleasure of being broad, collaborating and exchanging love with many friends. This heart will become bitter in its loneliness unless a challenge is presented that stretches it wide.

A third possibility is that your well-rounded heart needs an exceptional breadth at this time, to lead its growth further. Some dimension is always in the lead; it could be that this is the time for width to lead. This would be shown by an opportunity coming to you that requires you to be more of a "people person" than you've ever been, to work through others instead of being the main contributor, to trust others even when you have no history with them. If you can become broad-hearted you can succeed at such a challenge, but if not, you will have to decline the opportunity. All of these possibilities are very common.

Becoming Broad-Hearted

Even though our society has developed many excuse mechanisms to justify narrowness so that one need not feel guilty for it, it is still an unnatural condition, a weakness of heart, and a terrible confinement. People would naturally like to be broad-hearted, but wishing it alone is not sufficient; one must have a method. The intention to broaden the heart must be followed by a specific kind of attention to the heart and a method of supplying energy for the heart's growth. This can be done by the Heart Rhythm Meditation called "The Swinging Breath," described below, and practiced in everyday life by the "Exercises for Life" described later in this chapter.

Even if narrowness is not the issue for you at present, the basic practice used to make the heart wider is also the basis of the practices for some of the other dimensions.

Using Heart Rhythm Meditation

Monolithic Condition

Heart Rhythm Meditation has a powerful affect on the width of the heart. Each step in the practice is identified by a physical or emotional experience that acts as a milestone. The first we will aim for is a state called the "Monolithic Condition." This is a state of magnetic stillness with a clearly identifiable sensation that will provide feedback of your attainment of it. It is easy to learn, requiring between one week and one month of practice. When the Monolithic Condition is developed it has an immediate effect, producing calm and peacefulness, tolerance and accommodation of others, and an attitude of sympathy and helpfulness.

This technique must be practiced often. Real change in a person must come from real experience. When a person has genuine character, she is not dependent on remembering a set of platitudes, inspiring stories, or scriptures. When breadth of heart is genuine it is naturally sympathetic and kind; it cannot be otherwise. This comes through practice, not practice in politeness, which is a learned artificiality, but practice in putting attention on the heart, energizing the heart, listening to the heart, and making the heart active.

Posture for Heart Rhythm Meditation

First, find a posture that works. You can use a pillow, a bench, or a chair.

- If you use a pillow, you can either sit cross-legged on it or you can kneel and stuff it between your calves, to support your weight when you sit. If you're sitting cross-legged, be sure to have at least one knee on the floor. Otherwise the bottom of your spine will be bent.

- If you're using a bench, you can sit cross-legged or kneel and place it over your calves. You will automatically have your knees on the floor, and your lower back will be straight. If your knees hurt, you can add a cushion under your knees.

- If you're sitting in a chair, don't lean back; sit up with your spine absolutely vertical, like a pharaoh. The chair should be tall enough that your thighs are level or slightly downward sloping. The seat of the chair should not slope backwards; if it does, put a pillow at the back of the seat so that your thighs are level or even downward sloping from your lap.

Your posture should be:

Comfortable - In a chair, be careful that the edge of your chair doesn't cut your thighs too much. On a pillow, be careful that your knees are not being hurt.

Stable - You don't want to be balancing yourself by muscular exertion. If you're sitting up straight, it takes very little effort to hold that posture.

Straight - Your spine is a superconductor that will radiate the energy of your heart into the space around you, exactly like a TV transmitting antenna. Antennas are always vertical for maximum propagation of electromagnetic waves.

Majestic - That's the best word to describe the overall position. Your shoulders need to be back and down. This will open up the space needed for breathing and open up the chest so that the heart can reverberate. If you sit even a little bit slouched, you fold your body at the diaphragm and your breath is limited. If you have rounded shoulders, you are compressing your chest and the heartbeat will be diminished, like if you put your hand on a drum, so sit with your shoulders back, in a pose that is very majestic.

You'll want to develop at least two postures that you can comfortably maintain, so you can switch off between them as needed.

The Widening Breath

Rhythmic Breath

As you sit still, the only motion you'll notice in your body is your breath and your heartbeat. Of these two, the breath is much easier to notice; its sensation overwhelms the heartbeat as long as you're breathing in or out. After you notice your breath, you learn to control it in order to create a balanced rhythm.

The benefits of breathing consciously and rhythmically are many. First, the fact that your breath is conscious changes your neurological and muscular systems to use a different part of your brain to control a different set of muscles for breathing. This frees up a part of your unconscious mind that was busy with breathing, and that makes the power of the unconscious mind suddenly available. This phenomenon is so strong and reliable that meditators have always said there is no meditation without conscious breath.

Second, the regular rhythm of the Widening Breath creates a similar rhythm in the heartbeat, which is then broadcast to every cell in the body. The human body needs a regular rhythm to grow and maintain itself properly. This rhythm includes regular periods of activity and repose, waking and sleeping, eating and not eating, joy and solemnity, and inhaling and exhaling. The body has clocks within itself, and these clocks dictate the pace of metabolism, movement and even thinking. When the strongest and most basic rhythm in the body, the breath rhythm, becomes stable, the heartbeat adopts the rhythm too, and then the emotional state becomes calm.

Eight Steps

Here is the description of the Widening Breath, in eight steps. Do as many of these steps as you can now; with practice you'll be able to go further.

1.   Take a majestic posture with your hands on your legs.

2.   Make your breath conscious, breathing through your nose. Think of the earth spreading out below you. Feel rooted in it, part of it, adopting its steady stability.

3.   To make it easy to feel your pulse, press the fingertips of one hand into the center of your chest, just over the sternum. With the right amount of pressure, you will feel a pulsing in your fingertips, or a throbbing in your chest, or both. If you don't feel a pulse, then place your left hand over your heart and hook your left wrist with your right hand so that your right middle finger is over the artery underneath your left wrist. This is the spot nurses use to take your pulse.

4.   Place your hands back on your thighs. When you finish your in-breath, hold your breath for ten seconds or so and you may feel your heart throbbing in your chest. If not, you might feel your pulse somewhere else in your body. The pulse is the echo of the heartbeat -- notice where the pulse first appears. It could be in the end of your nose, your hands, your thighs, your temples, anywhere. If you concentrate, you can find it wherever you direct your attention, but where it appears spontane-

ously is very interesting. There's a message in it from your unconscious: "Look here!" Each part of the body has a meaning.

5.   Once you can feel either your pulse or your heartbeat, use that as a counting rhythm. If you still can't feel either pulse or heartbeat, then just count mentally, slowly. You will feel the pulse eventually. Count six heartbeats while breathing out and again six heartbeats while breathing in. If that's too fast, make it eight heartbeats. Don't hold your breath at all. Using your pulse or heartbeat as a rhythm links your breath rate to your heart rate and makes the inhale and exhale the same length.

6.   Imagine that your heart is breathing and that it draws its inhalation from the space to the left of you, and sends its exhalation to the space to the right of you. Take every breath this way: in on the left and out on the right.

7.   Imagine your breath makes a circle, where the breath exiting your right side passes in front of you and enters on your left side. In your imagination, place someone in front of you so that stream of breath passes through his or her heart. Let this person be someone who depends upon you or about whom you are concerned. Take several breaths this way until it becomes easy to imagine. Then add another person and keep breathing. Add more people and begin to include those of whom you feel intolerant. Let your breath pass through all their hearts on its path back to yourself.

8.   As you breathe in, repeat mentally to yourself, "I accept all that is given to me." As you breathe out, repeat mentally, "I give all that my heart does contain." Time one word with each heartbeat so that you breathe in for

eight heartbeats and out for eight heartbeats. These phrases replace the counting of heartbeats and add a universal, emotional dimension to the meditation.

Exercises for Life

As mentioned earlier, the Exercises for Life are designed to develop the dimensions of the heart, carrying the energy and inspiration gained from Heart Rhythm Meditation into life. To practice these exercises, read them over every day. One way to do that is to record them onto an audio tape or CD which you play in your car on your way to work. (We have also developed a number of meditation recordings, available at the IAM website, www.appliedmeditation.org.) Another way to keep these exercises before you is to type them up, frame them beautifully, and post them somewhere you look each day, like your refrigerator, or the wall of your office. (Our publisher has produced a beautiful set of these framed reminders, also available at the IAM website.) If you have a favorite among the set, repeat it before meals and before going to sleep. If you know others who are using the same exercises, you could meet together to discuss the exercises, their meaning and implications, and your successes with them.

These are exercises, and like any exercise, they give benefits according to how often they are repeated; they are never completed. We fail at these things, and we also succeed at them. Each exercise is designed to stretch your heart in one dimension, and these operate on the width of your heart.

Width, #1

> If there is anyone with whom you would not like to be alone in an elevator, that is your signal that a reconciliation is needed, for the health of your own heart. Take the initiative to resolve your differences with that person so you do not have to fear them or be embarrassed by them. This will bring peace and contentment.

When there is someone you try to avoid, that person defines the edge of the width of your heart. The narrowing of your heart will cost you in narrowed opportunities for friendships and alliances, a narrowed base of support that will leave you isolated in difficult times, and a narrow scope of influence. This cost accumulates as you get older and becomes so heavy a burden that no opportunity to resolve an old feud should be missed.

This first exercise can help you find the memory in your heart of the person you're avoiding, and the associated wound of resentment or guilt. Resentment occurs when someone does something to you that hurts you. Guilt occurs when you do something to someone else that hurts them, which then wounds your own heart as well. The memory of the original resentment or guilt is usually suppressed, so one has to do some emotional digging. The memory always has a face associated with it, and one can't bear to see that face, even though the heart yearns for resolution.

The avoidance of the person whose presence makes you uncomfortable can become so strong that you are not able to even recall that person. However, the discomfort is retained in the heart unconsciously. The heart is always trying to heal its wounds, so it will draw into your life, if not the person himself or herself, then a person who reminds you of him or her. Thus the discomfort spreads from the original person to a class of people with some similarity to that person, and this will result in some degree of social phobia, one of the most common psychological disorders.

Another version of this exercise is to consider who it might be that would ruin your party with their presence. If there is such a person, then it would be better for you to take a step toward reconciliation than for you to take a step back from their confrontation. The universe has a way of drawing back into your life whoever is needed to stretch your heart wider. Either you stretch willingly in resignation, or unwillingly in humiliation. It's worth a great deal to avoid the bitterness that comes from a narrow heart.

Lynn was fired by her boss and she felt bitter about it. When the axe fell, so to speak, Lynn felt she'd been scapegoated. The reasons she'd been given felt like a cover for her boss's real agenda: a vendetta against the person who had brought Lynn into the firm. Lynn suffered through a long period of job searching, followed by a placement at considerably less salary.

After a few years, Lynn settled into her new job and forgot about her former boss and the pain of her dismissal. Then one day when Lynn was lunching at her new favorite restaurant, she was startled to see her old boss pass by outside. Lynn hadn't been seen, she was sure, but still she choked on her sandwich. Immediately, all the old feelings she had around the time of her firing came up in her throat; she wasn't able to swallow or even speak. As a Heart Rhythm Meditator, she recognized the symptom as a cry for attention from her wounded heart. After that, she included in her meditations a time to think of her old boss with even breath and heartbeat sensation.

A year later, her son was preparing his college applications. She smiled when she saw that one of his favorites happened to be the alma mater of her old boss. She saw in this the opportunity to act in a healing way -- she called her old boss at home and said, "When I was working for you, you used to tell me that if my son ever wanted to apply to your alma mater I should let you know. Well, he is, and he could really use your help, since you have so many contacts there." Her old boss was quite moved and inquired about where she was working and if she'd landed on her feet. Lynn was able to joke about the past and even expressed gratitude, saying "Being hired and fired by you were two of the best events of my last decade."

Sometimes a person says they've forgotten something, but it's just under the surface, and it reappears during meditations or when touched by some event. To really forget the past is very difficult, and it's not really the goal; we want to be able to integrate all of life's experiences into our being, to take life's refuse and turn it into living, fertile earth, out of which life's bounty grows.

Do you have a strong digestion system? Can you take any food and turn it into nutrients? Very few people can. Much of what we eat passes through us without complete digestion, or sticks in our skin, fat, blood and organs in unhealthy ways. Similarly, what we experience in life we take into our heart, and this has to be absorbed and digested into life's wisdom. This process is called "assimilation," and it is generally as inefficient as our physical digestion.

The importance of assimilation is two-fold: First, it is necessary to keep the psyche healthy. If we do not assimilate something, we hold it as a regret, a resentment, or a confusion. "How could that person have done that?" "I cannot tolerate what has occurred." "I wish I had never done that." But when we have assimilated something we have truly learned it; it has become a part of us.

Second, assimilation is the process by which the whole universe learns through the experience of each of us. The One Being assimilates what we have each assimilated, and in this way humanity progresses.

Assimilation is done by breath. Heart Rhythm Meditation brings breath to the depth of the heart, a region very close to the stomach that performs physical digestion, stimulating your heart's 'emotional digestion'.

Kevin initiated divorce proceedings against his wife. The marriage hadn't gone well from his point-of-view, and he had become interested in another woman who was very comforting to him. From the time he told his wife he would be divorcing her, he had no further direct contact with her. His lawyer spoke to her lawyer, and the proceedings dragged on. The isolation deprived both Kevin and his wife of any resolution or processing of the grief of separation. For both of them, the other person was definitely the last one they would want to show up spontaneously at their party. But both had strong needs to see each other. She wanted to know what it was she did "wrong;" he wanted to know she was all right and didn't hate him.

After learning Heart Rhythm Meditation Kevin was able to initiate a meeting with his wife, in which he took responsibility for the breakup and asked her forgiveness, something he never thought he would be able to do. The divorce was concluded after that, so the relationship was not saved, but they do not avoid each other. They have occasional meetings through their common interests in which they enjoy each other's company and are respectful of each other. Still

to come is an honest and open review of what happened for both of them in their marriage and its disso-
lution.

Width, #2

> Mean what you say and say what you mean; speak
> clearly and simply. This will make you trustworthy.

Don't be vague, sarcastic or cute in your expression. If
you speak one word in ten, your words mean much more.

The elated-hearts like to use words to lift the atmosphere when things are too serious. The deep hearts use words
to probe and comfort. The forward hearts may use words to
provoke and confront others. These are all valuable forms of
expression, but the heart that is wide uses words in a different
way, and those who want to widen their hearts would do well
to adopt this way.

Realizing that words have a great power, you never
want to allow words to escape your lips that say the opposite
of what you mean, even in jest. The objective is to be able to
express your heart in everything you say. Of course, an expression from your heart would never be deceitful or insincere. The ability to control your speech shows the ability to
control your emotions.

Sam has developed the social defense of "banter,"
where the objective of conversation is to toss an idea
back-and-forth between opposing points of view to
see how long you can keep it in the air. Whatever
position the other person starts with, say, the failures
of the war in Iraq, Sam will take the opposite side and
argue it convincingly until his conversational oppo-
nent changes his tack. If he hears agreement, then he
shifts his stance to stay on the offensive. In the discussion of one topic, he might make many points on both

sides, which he considers to be essential to an unbiased search for the truth. Although his friends regard him as clever, they would also say he is unprincipled. You never know what Sam really thinks; he lacks conviction and integrity.

Kyle has the habit of making snide remarks, followed by, "Just kidding." If people object to his sarcasm and belittling, he admonishes them for taking offense at a joke. Like Sam, Kyle says much more than needs to be said, without adding meaning and without thoughtful consideration of the topic or the feelings of the person he's speaking to. When heart speaks, it speaks to the heart of another, but Sam and Kyle are not speaking from their heart, and their words are discounted, ignored or resented.

Stuart says less than most people, but what he says is sincere. When he speaks, people stop talking and listen. His remarks often change the direction or tone of the conversation. His friends appreciate his contributions and seek out his opinions. He says one word in ten, but his one word counts as a hundred words of insincere chatter.

Width, #3

> When you give your word to someone, consider that you are bound to that person until they agree to release you from your commitment. This will make you dependable.

Break not your word of honor whatever may befall. Your word is your bond. By holding your commitment to your word, even when it is inconvenient, you create stability in life; not just your own life, but the lives of all those you touch will benefit from your stability. Your discipline will create safety for others, which they will return to you as trust. The fact that keeping one's word is a rare behavior makes it all the more valuable. By practicing this you will give the impression to others that you are responsible: capable of holding a great weight upon your shoulders. It won't be simply an impression; your heart will develop that width that makes stability and dependability possible.

Laura said she would attend the planning meeting, but then the development committee scheduled a meeting at the same time. She asked to be excused from the planning meeting, but the others involved couldn't make her suggested alternative times. The leader of the planning meeting told her they would all be disappointed if she didn't come, but Laura had a friend that assured her they would get over it and she should do what she wants to do. As much as Laura would like to be able to miss the planning meeting to attend the development meeting, she realizes the cost of breaking a commitment is too great in terms of her perceived loyalty and dependability. People had juggled their calendars to attend the planning meeting because they knew she would be there. While the organizer of development committee was disappointed, he knew this meant that when Laura gave her word to him, he would receive the same dependability she was showing toward the planning committee meeting.

It is very sobering to think that you have to keep a commitment just because you made it. The only release from a commitment is to follow through, or be excused by the person or persons to whom the commitment was made. This is an uncommon, noble way to behave, a natural expression of the heart, to which one's commitment is actually made.

Width, #4

> Look at things from another person's point-of-view. Your own point-of-view will not be lost, but your view of reality will be widened.

When people aggravate us we ridicule their point-of-view, imagining them to be stupid or unreasonable. The last thing we want is to see things the way that awful person sees them -- that seems like taking a mental poison! Yet people are rarely stupid or unreasonable; we brand them that to insulate ourselves from their thinking. Thinking can be right or wrong, but the heart can only be right. We deprive ourselves of wisdom by closing our minds, and worse, the belittling of another closes our heart.

If you have the courage to try to see things through another's eyes, you will be rewarded by better sight. One point-of-view cannot see the complex reality accurately. It is a mind trap to fall into one's own opinion, a symptom of a shallow heart. Those who are obstinate in their opinions are to be pitied, not blamed. It is their own heart's weakness reflected in their mind's eye and it will limit their freedom and happiness in life. There is no danger in taking another's point-of-view; if it expands you, you can keep it and be benefited, and if it constricts you, you can discard it.

Gertrude lives in the country next to a farmer that raises free-running chickens. Gertrude had just spent $200 on plants for her garden, and the chickens scratched around and dug them up. She was angry and sent her husband next door to talk to the farmer about getting rid of his chickens or paying for a better fence. The neighbor just stared at Gertrude's husband

and said he would no such thing. Gertrude felt like calling the police or killing the chickens herself, but before doing either of these things, she spent some time in Heart Rhythm Meditation contemplating her neighbor. She remembered how she previously had been close to the family next door. The man's wife had been ill for years and the man had provided constant care for his wife, with few diversions, until she died.

Gertrude moved into his point of view and saw how the chickens were his only joy, representing health, happiness and freedom which he no longer had in his own life. By seeing the situation this way, she felt ashamed of her egotistic view and decided it would please her to plant some sturdy things that chickens could eat and not destroy, plant some other things that chickens did not like, put fences around some of her plants, and renew her earlier friendship with her neighbor. She realized the heart never wishes for separation and always longs for re-union, and she had missed having him as a friend.

Fred has been a peace activist since his college days during the Vietnam War. He instinctively reacts against militaristic solutions to world problems. He has also been a radical Christian who finds support for his pacifism in the teachings of Jesus. It was obvious to him that he could not vote for George Bush, who had led the country into war. Fred's cousin, who was also a committed Christian, was a strong supporter of the president. Fred could become extremely agitated arguing with his cousin; his contempt for his cousin's views was so extreme that no one could stand to be in the same room with them when they were talking politics. Fred realized his family relationships were suffering from his intolerance, but he felt the power of righteousness.

He used Heart Rhythm Meditation to reach the depth of his heart and the place of connection to his cousin. Then he felt his cousin's idealism, as strong as his own, and realized that his cousin saw in George Bush a champion of the unborn child, a pacifism of a different kind. Although the ideal was different, it was just as heart-felt, and no amount of rational argument would touch it, just as his non-militaristic views were rooted in his own heart. He saw that both he and his cousin emphasized an aspect of compassion, and in their dedication to compassion their hearts could meet.

Width, #5

> When the lack of focus, initiative, persistence or success of others around you annoys you, take this as a signal that you need to improve your own self-mastery through concentration on some specific, personal goal.

When the lack of self-mastery of others annoys you, it is probably because they remind you of some lack of self-mastery in yourself. Perhaps you've been struggling with excessive weight, lack of physical fitness, inability to keep to a schedule, losing your temper, or taking offense too easily. Your frustration can be aggravated by others who don't even seem to be trying to improve themselves. Or perhaps you've given up attaining some aspect of your self-mastery, like a goal for your own weight, and so you've forgotten how hard people struggle with themselves. Either way, the solution is to choose a realistic goal and dedicate yourself to it. Direct toward yourself all that annoyance you feel toward others. Your judgment of others is a sign that you need to more strictly judge yourself.

Steve found himself withdrawing from his family. He didn't understand why his son escaped into computer games, why his daughter was getting such poor marks in school, or why his wife kept the television running all evening. Steve felt assaulted by the noise of the TV, the games, and his daughter's incessant phone calls. He expressed his annoyance frequently in criticism of everyone else, and, as that was rebuffed, he withdrew from them more and more.

Steve's Heart Rhythm Meditation gave him another view of his life: he felt how powerless he was in controlling his weight. He couldn't resist extra helpings of dinner; he had rather quickly gained 20 pounds, and now couldn't get them off. He was anxious about his work and his general state-of-mind and he saw his personal failings mirrored in those around him. With the encouragement of his Heart Rhythm mentor, he resolved to present a personal example of self-control and success to his family. As he fought with his life-long propensity toward over-eating, he became much more tolerant and forgiving of the lapses of others. He shared his internal battle, with its humbling setbacks and inspiring advances, and this moved his family much more than his former criticism of them had.

Width #6

> Consider what is expected of you by all those with whom you come in contact and try to answer their demands to the best of your ability, willingly, and patiently. Give something to each person, as generously as possible, choosing the level at which you give: physically, mentally, emotionally, or spiritually.

The path of the heart is not the path of freedom; it is the path of responsibility. There are many who depend upon you: some for a smile, a greeting, an insight. Some need you to pull your weight, others need you to pull them. You provide energy, leadership, security, and love to some, and receive the same from others. Your heart is part of a network of hearts that circulates the energy of love through humanity, and you are a vital link in that network. Whatever you can contribute to others will circulate and return to you augmented.

Sometimes people ask more of you than you can manage to give. In these cases, you can give at a higher level.

Often, your physical presence is wanted, but when you cannot appear in person you can give your idea. Many people want your personal, hands-on effort -- give as much of it as you can, and then give your advice to a wider group. When you are asked for a fish, first give as many fish as you can, and second, teach fishing.

If there are many who seek your knowledge, then give as much advice as you can. But if there are more than you can respond to, then before your mind is exhausted, give your blessing and encouragement instead.

When there are many who depend on your encouragement, send your prayers to those whose hearts you cannot lift directly. There is no limit to the scope of this level of giving, and it is an obligation of every person to seek the well-being of the whole of humanity.

Width #7

> When you possess something, think of the one who does not possess it. This will make you considerate and thankful.

There is no blame in accumulating possessions and wealth in general. Sometimes wealth makes a person grateful and generous, and sometimes wealth makes a person stingy and protective. The former is broad, the latter, narrow. How can you avoid becoming narrow-hearted with your wealth? By this exercise of considering the ones who do not have what you have.

This exercise is not narrowly moralistic; it neatly side-steps the questions of how you acquired what you have, whether by luck, effort, or some form of exploitation, and the question of whether you deserve to have it. It focuses on the very fact that you have more than others have, and in that unequal distribution of the earth's resources, there is an obligation that you will have to address in some way.

What people usually do is the opposite of this exercise -- when they don't have something, they think of the ones who do have it, and this makes them discontent, envious, and unappreciative.

We know a man who was very successful in business, though he came from a very unsuccessful family. His father was poor, and supported the family partly through petty crime. The father's attitude was, "Why should that person have so much while I have so little?" The parents were devoted Catholics, hopeful that their confession at the end of their lives would result in absolution of a lifetime of crime. They were determined that in spite of their poverty, their son would attend the best Catholic college in the area, Boston College, and he did. Our friend told us how his father had called him one day in college and asked him to help him with a job, an armed robbery of a convenience store, because the father was desperate for money, and how he did it with his father, one last time.

When he graduated from Boston College, he was hired by a local manufacturer, where he rose to eventually become the CEO. When the company was sold, his stock was worth millions. He started a new company, and hired among a large staff a few of his old friends from his old neighborhood, or their sons. He hosted his parents at his large and prestigious home, or his townhouse, or his farm, without concern for what his wealthy friends thought of them. He married a cook at the cafeteria of his old company and put a million dollars in her private account so that she could be assured of a secure future, whether their marriage lasted or not. He gave generously to Boston College and to organizations working in his family's neighborhood.

The most beautiful thing about him, we always felt, was the soft humility that came over him when he thought of his early life. He had achieved respect and fortune by his own efforts, yet he felt that the grace of God was a large factor, in spite of his unworthiness, and that he had an obligation to those who hadn't received such grace.

John was from an old New England family that inherited a great deal of wealth from a ship captain two hundred years ago. He was candid about the source of his ancestor's money: "He ran the triangle trade, taking rum to Africa, where he traded it for slaves, whom he took to the West Indies where he traded them for sugar cane, which he then brought to Boston to be distilled into rum. Basically, he was a slaver, though he had the prestige and wealth of a ship captain, who were some of the most admired men of their time."

Although John never had to work for income, he worked hard his whole life, first in Kennedy's Peace Corps, then in various startups devoted to improving the environment, then in social services organizations. His family's wealth was deep and wide and could have offered him the life of royalty, but he preferred to be in contact with those whom he could help.

Width #8

> Identify yourself with someone else, to remove the assumptions you make about who you must be and what role you must play. Try thinking of yourself as a teacher, an animal, a leader, a man, a woman, a humble saint, etc. In this way you will come to appreciate the qualities and strengths of others, and gain them for yourself.

By exercising your ability to consciously identify with whatever you wish, you will purify yourself of the unconscious identity you have assumed, which is circumstantial, not essential.

There is a tendency for an actor to become identified with his role. We are all actors, playing a role in the drama of life, and we all have more breadth than our role allows. However, we can't be aware of this breadth until we step outside of our role. We assume that men have to act a certain way, and women a different way. This is a conventionality created by the society to make our lives easier to perform. But with a limited role, we become as narrow as we are cast. There is a natural motivation in us to expand our role, but our identity becomes fixed over time and we lose flexibility and spontaneity.

In order to discover your wider range of thinking and behavior you can think of yourself as someone else. Your own idea of who you are is so limited by the role in which you've specialized that you cannot free yourself from your own typecasting. Part of the appeal of the stage is that the actor gets a chance to explore a different character. This is so valuable an experience that it shouldn't be limited to the theater.

Roger used this method of widening his heart. In the morning he would go to his jar of roles and pick out a small piece of folded paper that might say, "Saint," "Millionaire," "Student," "Newspaper Reporter," "Visitor from another Planet," "Woman disguised as a man," etc. Then he'd adopt that attitude and style for the whole day. His role started as soon as he left the house, and he'd try to stay in character all day. He'd buy his paper in that role, and he'd start up conversations on the train in his role. He'd read his paper through the eyes of his character, and he'd try to adapt his gait to the way his character would walk. His conversations at work would take on that tone, although no one would know. His identity was internal, not external, yet it affected the way people would respond to him.

Roger found that by adopting different roles, he was able to access a broader range of approaches and become more successful. The situation that was closed to the "Millionaire" might be open to the "Newspaper Reporter." The openness of the "Student," who is not afraid to ask questions and makes no assumptions of knowing anything, often results in new discoveries. But some situations require the bearing and confidence of the "Millionaire."

After practicing in this way for many months, Roger found that he could shift from one role to another in the situation, as needed. The width of his heart encompassed all these possibilities.

The practice of imagining oneself as someone else is a great advantage in learning to do something that you don't think you can do. For example, if you've tried meditation and find you can't do it, try imagining that you are your meditation teacher. This works best with a real, live meditation teacher you know personally.

Chapter 5

Reaching the
Depth of the Heart

5. Reaching the Depth of the Heart

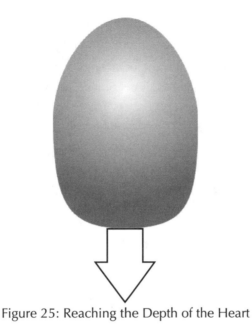

Figure 25: Reaching the Depth of the Heart

This Chapter

Here we present a meditation, called the Downward Breath, and eight Exercises for Life that call you into the depth of your heart, beginning the development of the vertical dimension of the heart, which continues in Chapter 6.

The Beauty of the Depth

The depth of your heart is its most precious and vulnerable place. It is here, at the solar plexus, just below the ribcage, that the heart feels the greatest and most transpersonal emotions: unconditional love, inconsolable sorrow, unspeakable bliss, unending communion with all life. In short, the symphony of cosmic emotions that J.S. Bach expressed in the Mass in B Minor is here in the depth of your heart all the time. Occasionally something happens to create an access point to one of these great emotions and it rises toward the surface of the heart where it becomes more conscious.

In the depth of your heart you experience the whole human experience, before it becomes translated into your personal version of that experience. Here are the common roots of the lily pads, far below the surface in the fertile soil of all being.

Most people don't come to their depth, even though this is a place of great emotion and love, because the entry price is passing through the portal of the conscience where one must face the two guard dogs, resentment and guilt. Resentment is your feeling that others have harmed you, and guilt is your feeling that you have harmed others.

Using Heart Rhythm Meditation

The Downward Breath

The Breath of Water

The Downward Breath simulates a waterfall as it causes a stream of energy to flow downward to and through your heart. We use the Downward Breath to access the depth of the heart and to awaken the qualities of a deep heart: compassion, connectedness, empathy and sincerity.

Eight Steps

Here are the eight steps of this meditation; go as far as you are able, then go farther with more practice.

1. Sit up straight and put your hand on your heart. Immediately your energy field changes as your hand's position draws your attention to your heart. You could put your palm over the middle of your chest, the "heart cen-

ter," or you could touch the heart center with your fingertips. You can use either hand.

2. Breathe in through your nose and out through your mouth. Let your exhalation be like a fine stream, a gentle blowing. Close your mouth as you breathe in, and open it as you breathe out again. Start the Downward Breath like a silent sigh, then extend it a few more seconds. Make your breath rhythmic, alternating in and out without a pause.

3. Look for your heartbeat or pulse, as you did in the last chapter's "Widening Breath."

4. Coordinate your breath with your heartbeat, counting six heartbeats while you inhale and the same number for exhale. When you can keep this rhythm for about ten breaths in a row, lengthen your breath to eight heartbeats in and eight out.

5. As you breathe in, think of your breath as a stream of life that descends from above. Draw the water down into your heart. As you breathe out, let the stream pass down, through you, with no resistance, flowing down your legs and out your feet, and also flowing out from the bottom of your spine and out of your palms.

6. While you breathe this way, think of the basic characteristics of water: its direction is downward, its nature is fluid, its color is green.[22] Think of yourself the same way: let yourself become fluid, flexible and graceful like a being of water.
    Emotionally, the Downward Breath gives a great release and relief. It fills the holes in your heart and completes

---

[22] Bair (2007) Chapter 12, describes this practice as the Water Breath.

your emotions as it recharges your heart with new energy. For example, the Downward Breath resolves anger, which is an incomplete emotion about yourself, by completing it with compassion for others.

7. Focus on the flow of breath through your heart. As you breathe out, your breath descends deeper into your heart, accompanied by deeper emotion and a sense of willing and grateful surrender. As you continue this breath for at least five minutes, you'll find your emotion gets deeper and deeper. Many people report the feeling that something descends upon them; most feel that their heart is touched; some feel a great and powerful emotion of love.

Spiritually, water is the metaphor for love. Just as water is the element that cleanses physically, so love is the element that purifies emotionally. Love's stream is so powerful that it dissolves the painful impressions of a lifetime as it fills your heart with admiration and respect for all.

8. Feel the heart's emotion as a deep pool of pure emotional energy. In the depth of the heart the emotions arise without a cause except for the breath itself. (Emotions closer to the surface of everyday consciousness need a trigger -- like some evocative image of suffering, a memory of pure joy, a piece of music, or the touch of a sensation that is linked to an emotion.) As your emotions arise, they are released and you descend even farther into the safety, stillness and peace in the depth of the lake of your heart, a place that is unaffected by the winds at the surface.

Exercises for Life

These Exercises for Life can be practiced anytime, to develop the depth of the heart.

Depth, #1

> See yourself reflected in another. See how that person is similar to you. See how they become more similar as you feel more accommodation, respect, admiration and love for them.

It's easy to see the differences in people. Our vision supports this view: we look different, so we must be different. Further, since we can't change our appearances to all look alike, our differences must also be immutable. Much of our human interactions are based on these two concepts: (1) people are different, and (2) that difference does not change. But beneath appearances, we are amazingly alike, and we are all in a constant state of change.

Being able to see the differences between people is smart, but being able to see the similarities is wise. It is smart to avoid the assumption that others will think or do what you would do. But it's wise to feel some similarity with another because that is your point of contact, the beginning of your relationship. From this feeling of similarity, your closeness will grow and you will both change. Difference is perceived by the mind; similarity is felt with the heart.

One way to begin to develop this feeling of similarity is to imagine that the other person reflects yourself back to yourself. When you are competitive, the other person becomes more competitive. When you are kind, the other is also more kind. The reflection has many imperfections: people's hearts are usually not capable of being perfectly reflective, due to their own wounds. Still, the principle holds and you can gain a great insight into yourself by looking for your reflection in others.

What might be surprising is that by finding your reflection in someone, which reveals a similarity between you, you cause a shift in that person that moves them toward a greater similarity. Whereas the perception of difference causes a reinforcement of difference, the perception of similarity causes a surrender of difference. The influence you can have on a different person is like the outside influence you have on an object, while the influence you have on a similar person is like the inside influence you have on yourself. Everyone is both different and similar to you; you can see it either way, if your heart is strong enough. If you can feel any similarity, then you can build respect and admiration on that, which will draw you closer and reveal even more of your reflection in your friend's heart.

Richie owned a restaurant in Manhattan. He had many employees working for him, and he did all the hiring and firing. One of the people he had hired as waiter, Matt, was a skilled waiter, but he was chronically late to work. Just as Richie was ready to fire Matt because of his inability to be punctual, Richie's mother came to see her son at the restaurant in Manhattan for her yearly visit. Matt was her waiter and the mother fell in love with him. She thought that he was the restaurant's best waiter! When Richie disclosed the problems he'd had with Matt being tardy, his mother reminded Richie of how, in his own youth, he had been unable to get up in the morning and had frequently been late to his own shifts. Richie remembered those early years and how he had gone on to become a great waiter himself. He started a new approach with Matt: he saw Matt as an younger version of himself. Richie tried to remember how he overcame his morning sleepiness, and he began to coach Matt like an older brother instead of a boss. Matt immediately felt the difference in approach, and was touched that Richie would take an interest in him. Richie saw even more of himself in Matt as Matt responded to him just as Richie had responded to his early mentor. Matt arrived at work on time, but that was a minor change compared to the new relationship that had developed.

Depth, #2

> Feel another person. People are very different than they appear and even different than they think they appear. Your feeling of another tells you more than their words and actions can.

Ralph started and ran his own business, which grew over the years to become quite successful. He naturally thought of himself as a powerful and accomplished person. However, he couldn't make his marriage work. He applied all he had learned from his successful work to the cause of improving his relationship, but the more effort he put into it, the worse it got.

At a seminar, his Heart Rhythm teacher surprised him by identifying the depth of Ralph's heart as his natural heart quality, where Ralph had assumed it was the forward direction, due to his growing business. He then realized that he was not actually comfortable with the energy of pushing; he much preferred to just support his customers well and let them expand his reputation and therefore his business. He had made his business grow not by his sales effort, but by his responsiveness; not by power, but by love.

He decided to apply this method to his marriage -- he stopped treating it like a project that had to be managed and instead listened for the dissatisfaction he had not heard. He was responsive to his wife, and she responded to him. The breakthrough came from the insight that he was actually a deeply empathetic person who had learned to behave in an aggressive manner that he thought was necessary in the world. His business success had come in spite of his attempts to be tough; he was successful when he used his true strength of understanding.

Some people are brought up to behave a certain way that is quite different from their nature. For example, for a long time women have been taught to be submissive and not assertive, gentle and graceful. But half of the women in the world have hearts that would have been better suited in a body and psyche of power and courage. And men have been taught traditionally to take risks and be assertive, to be disciplined and focused, even though half of all men have hearts that are better suited to a style of harmony and compassion.

For many people, the experiences of life are so contrary to their nature that they deny their sensitive and sacred qualities to create a defensive armor. Some others find life so confusing that they cannot bring out their power without causing hurt and more confusion in others. If the roles and rules of society are too rigid, or the circumstances of life are too harsh and chaotic, many people will not have the opportunity to explore and develop their true nature, trying instead to apply the methods that other people have used.

You do a great service to your friends if you can feel their heart's dimensions directly instead of assuming their heart's nature is the same as their demeanor. It is the depth of your heart that gives you the empathy needed to sense the dimensions of another's heart.

Depth, #3

> Identify what irritates you about yourself when you see it reflected in another. Recognize that it is your own emerging quality you see in the one you admire.

The most irritating thing that others do to you is to reflect your deficiency back to yourself. There are two ways this happens: some people, through their success, remind you of your failures. This is envy, and it hurts you most when you are already aware of your lack, like salt in a wound. Others show you a quality you admire in yourself, but they distort or disregard the quality. This is sacrilege, trampling on something you hold in high regard. Some examples will clarify:

(Envy) Tom and Mary worked together in the same department, and both hoped to gain the position of department head someday. When a vacancy finally occurred in the position, Tom was picked over Mary. Mary was bitter about the decision, and just seeing Tom's face was distressing to her. She knew why he had been chosen: he was much better at building alliances with other parts of the company, while she had worked on becoming more productive and creative at the job they had shared. It was unfair, she thought, to promote the less skilled, but she also realized that her greater skill meant she was more valuable where she was. That was a logical argument she could accept; what really aggravated her was that Tom's ability to communicate and build relationships with others at his new level was something she wanted to be able to do and just couldn't. Her nerves

153

didn't allow it. Her anger at Tom was really anger at herself, the most frustrating and common kind of anger. Fortunately, every heart has intrinsically the ability to communicate and relate openly, and Mary can develop this skill by practice. Heart Rhythm Meditation will give her the confidence to calm her nerves and be relaxed among others. Already, she's benefitted by knowing that the skill she sees in Tom must also be in herself, though temporarily buried under fear.

(Sacrilege) Harold's father was a powerful man, in charge at the First National bank, in charge of the city's most influential fraternal group, and in charge at home. He did not like being talked back to, and he expected his orders to his son to be carried out exactly. Being frequently disciplined by his father had developed in Harold a strong dislike for authority. Harold became the family rebel, a clown to his father's seriousness and an embarrassment to his father's pride. Harold was his father's son, with all the same potential and capacity for power, but because Harold had so much exposure to the oppressive side of power, he denied his own. It was not until Harold met Damian that he was able to take his first steps towards leadership and responsibility. Damian used Heart Rhythm Meditation to stay in touch with his heart and consequently he was able to be persevering, self-confident and courageous while maintaining kindness, tolerance and generosity. Damian's example was a revelation to Harold; he had never known a man could be both strong and open at the same time. Damian taught him that the ability to be open hearted was the greatest strength, that both compassion and courage were qualities of the heart and both could develop together and reinforce each other. Encouraged by Damian's model, and powered by the breath in his own heart, Harold was able to reclaim the best parts of his father's emotional inheritance.

It is sacrilege when a quality of one person's heart, in the above case, the power latent in Harold, is inhibited by the distortion of that same quality in another. It is infuriating when we see someone misuse that which we long to develop ourselves. Politicians who mislead and deceive, for example, cause many who would make great leaders to be cynical about public service and reject the political arena where they could have fulfilled their potential.

Working with the depth of the heart is important to overcome the preconceptions, fears and judgments that restrict us. In the depth of the heart we are all so much alike, sharing the same emotions, basic needs and aspirations. The hopeful message from Heart Rhythm Meditation is that whatever quality you see in another, whether in a pure or distorted form, is a quality your own heart possesses as well. The anger you see in another reminds you of your own power, and teaches you to express it consciously. The laziness you see in another reminds you of your own longing for peace.

(Sacrilege) Gwen always hated the ladies at the beach. Their self-indulgent laziness disgusted her. Gwen worked hard, too hard, and had no time for leisure. She felt completely justified in her judgments of those who had so much free time that they could literally lie in the sun, an activity that contributed nothing to the great needs of our time. But her prejudice aggravated her too; she wanted to understand the intensity behind it. Meditating on her heart, she discovered that her intense work schedule was driven by the belief that she could only be worthy of the respect and love of others if she produced at an extraordinary level. She actually longed to be able to relax without guilt, at least once in a while. The ladies at the beach were able to do it, without the encumbrance of guilt for what they weren't accomplishing. But to Gwen, they were over-doing it, distorting the valuable quality of self-care into "don't-care." Fearing that her own relaxation would snowball into apathetic hedonism, she had been denying herself the simple pleasure of rest she so needed. Her heart guided her to the solution: if she respected her heart, the source of her creativity and energy, she had to respect her heart's natural rhythm of activity and repose, and make time for free-time.

This exercise also helps us remember the qualities of our heart nature that we have forgotten and buried. You cannot appreciate a quality in another that is foreign to you. Even under stress and neglect, your heart still has the ability to draw into your life those people who are able to reflect what your heart feels as its own quality. Your response of admiration for another is your own recognition of your heart. Consider the confidence and grace of the people you know, and be assured that you wouldn't be able to value them if you did not see something in them that was already familiar in yourself.

The light-hearted are drawn to other light-hearted people, even when they are feeling heavy.

Claudia loved her friend Alice because of the tremendous generosity Alice consistently showed to her. Not only did she give her lovely presents, but she offered time when Claudia needed her, especially after Claudia's baby was stillborn and the long and difficult period of grieving which followed. Claudia wondered why she was so fond of Alice, her best friend. In Heart Rhythm Meditation Claudia was able to see that Alice's generosity appealed to her because this had been the quality in herself which became buried by her loss. Being with Alice was a reassuring memory of the qualities she would enjoy again when she felt whole.

Glenn was a creative type; his boss, Richard, was a numbers guy. Glenn came up with the program content while Richard made the company successful with Glenn's creations. Glenn loved his work, but he was intrigued with the way Richard was able to manage many employees and clients simultaneously even with ever-present financial worries. Glenn saw Richard as a king among men -- he didn't get discouraged; he could handle stress with nobility; he inspired confidence in others. Glenn was brilliant and dynamic, yet he admired Richard's qualities more than his own.

When one of their clients demanded full-time attention from Glenn, Glenn decided to strike out on his own. He formed a new company and found himself in his old boss's position. To Glenn's amazement, the qualities of the confident and responsible leader began to emerge in himself. He raised money, called on prospects, negotiated contracts, supervised delivery, counseled clients at informal evening meetings, all things that he'd never imagined he could do. When he was speaking about his old boss one day, his Heart Rhythm mentor told him, "You couldn't have seen Richard as a kingly type if you didn't feel the same within yourself." One day he realized he had become his own version of his mentor Richard, and of that he was prouder than any specific accomplishment.

Depth, #4

> Practice forgiveness, thereby demonstrating how the heart operates most naturally. Forgiveness can be practiced as tolerance, overlooking, and forgetting.

"Overlooking" in this case means to see but not to notice. It is similar to tolerance, which means to have the capacity to endure something or someone unpleasant, but in overlooking, you don't allow yourself to think about it. Forgetting carries overlooking one step farther: you erase the memory of the event from your heart.

(Tolerance) Caroline had dated Porter for three years when she became pregnant. When she told Porter the news, he said he was absolutely not ready to be a father and provided her with money for an abortion. Caroline had the abortion because she did not want to bring a child into a life where it was not wanted, but she suffered terribly from the termination of her pregnancy. Her despair overwhelmed her love for Porter; a month after the abortion she disconnected from him entirely.

Her abortion became a theme in Caroline's breathing practice, where she was able to remain aware of her feelings and tolerate the grief she felt due to the loss of both a child and a partner. Heart Rhythm Meditation didn't allow her to escape from these feelings, rather it made all her emotions very present in a much larger emotional heart that has the capacity to hold them.

A year later, Caroline ran into Porter on the subway. She was shocked and her heart leapt in surprise. She immediately thought of the rejection and loneliness she felt at the time of her pregnancy, but she was able to connect with her heart in that moment, and her heart had accepted that her ex-lover had a different attitude than she did about parenthood. Caroline looked into his eyes and said "Hi Porter, how are you?" He seemed surprised and pleased to meet her again. They had a cup of coffee together and caught up on the year since their relationship had ended. They found they were able to be friends.

(Overlooking) Mollie and Sage were house guests at Keith's, and had stayed out later than they had expected. When they arrived back at Keith's house, they found the house dark and all the doors locked. They rang the bell, feeling angry with themselves and sorry about abusing their privilege as house guests. Finally, they heard someone approach the door, and it was Keith in his robe. It was obvious that he had been sleeping. "We are so sorry we got you up." Keith was not bothered; he just wanted to calm the hearts of his guests, so he said, "No problem, I was just coming downstairs to check the door."

(Overlooking) Sue and Joe had worked in the same office for several years. Joe had a habit of borrowing writing utensils from Sue and not returning them. Sue went through dozens of pens and pencils over the time they knew each other. She did not say anything about it; she just bought more pens and pencils. One day, Joe said: "Sue, I have so many pens on my desk, do you need any?"

(Forgetting) Robert took a job as VP of Development for a robotics company. On his first day, he realized that the CEO was deliberately lying to the board, vastly overstating his own academic record, the capability of the robot, and the potential for commercial applications. Robert continued on, addressing the problem by redesigning the robot's weakest component, its computer. When Robert was ready to begin installation of the new computer, the CEO blocked the changes which he thought would delay his schedule. Robert told the CEO the changes would save the project, not delay it. At this, the CEO fired him rather than risk exposure, and then began an intensive campaign to discredit Robert so that no one would consider his arguments. Robert couldn't get another job in the robotics field, and switched careers a year later. The robotics company later failed. Asked by a friend, "What was the name of that CEO you used to work for in R&D," Robert replied, "Honestly, I don't remember." The friend, incredulous, asked, "How is it possible you could have forgotten the name of a man who ruined your career in robotics?" Robert said simply, "I didn't feed that memory with attention and it died of starvation." "How could you avoid thinking of him," the friend asked. "I fed my heart with a breathing practice I do, and the great emotion it causes to flow in my heart washed away any bitterness I had."

Depth, #5

> Reveal your innermost being with dignity; by so doing, you teach others how the heart operates.

The way the heart works is a mystery to most people, who think boundaries and privacy give emotional protection and their personality can hide what they feel. The truth is that people are highly intuitive and quickly sense an emotional coverup as something unnatural. "There's something odd about him," they'll say, "he's not what he appears to be." When you are comfortable within the depth of your heart, you know that openness creates emotional connections with people, and these bonds offer a greater security than hiding your feelings. The fear of being rejected is likely to cause rejection. Being open with people can lead to powerful alliances.

Mona was yelling at her daughter, Monique, for coming home late again on Saturday night. Mona worked at a prominent manufacturing company and was noted for being reliable, quiet, productive and able to handle enormous stress in the workplace. Her colleagues would have thought she was completely competent in her private life as well. With Monique though, she was inconsistent, controlling, and frequently angry whenever her daughter challenged the arbitrary limits her mother set. Mona was fearful that something would happen to Monique and her fears rose to irrational levels late at night. She kept her fears hidden from everyone who knew her, except Monique. Mona began attending Heart Rhythm Meditation classes and was able to look within herself at the two sides of her life which were so disconnected. Over time, she opened up more to people at work about her fears and the challenges of raising a teenager, made more friends, and was able to negotiate more effectively with Monique as well.

Elisabeth was intelligent, very capable, and had been at the firm a long time. It was no surprise to anyone that she rose through the ranks to Chief Investment Officer. She lured Tom, a well-known broker, from a competitor, which was a major accomplishment and success for the firm. But Tom was meticulous, and he was dismayed to see Elisabeth's office on his first day. There was nowhere to sit down; every chair was stacked with papers. She left only a small trail, wide enough to walk to her desk, over the floor that was otherwise piled with files. Her desk was layered like an archeological site, with papers and objects intermixed, age corresponding to depth. Tom suddenly understood why all his interviews with her had occurred in restaurants. But Elisabeth put him at ease immediately, and turned his contempt to admiration by saying, "I have a learning disability, Tom, that I've had to cope with all my life. I just can't handle files; I need to have everything out where I can see it." Her admission of her own flaw showed Tom that she appreciates the differences in people and is willing to judge by results rather than style.

Peter was the founder and Executive Director of a non-profit with a mission. He was a dynamic visionary and his enthusiasm and conviction attracted many to the organization. Sally wanted to sign on, but as she looked into the office procedures, she saw that accounting was lax, and that made her very uncomfortable. She wondered if Peter was covering up financial irregularities. Confronting him about her concerns, she expected him to defend against any criticism of his "baby," and resolved to leave quickly if he did. What Peter said, though, brought Sally on board and began a long and rewarding career: "Sally, with all of our success, there are parts of the organization that are not working. I very much need your help, as a partner in this great cause, and I'll be completely open with you about any detail of our operation. I hope you will help us fix it."

Depth, #6

> Let your heart be moved by the beauty and tragedy all around you.

When your heart is energized, the world becomes a much more beautiful place, and the tragedies of life become even more tragic. It's like watching a full-color movie when you're used to black and white -- everything seems more real than it did before. Without an energized heart, you couldn't stand it -- you'd have to turn down reality by fleeing into your mind, which filters out anything it can't understand. With your heart open and strong, you see beauty and tragedy, both, right in front of you and at distances previously inconceivable.

Jennifer was walking on the beach, enjoying the natural beauty of the surf, sand, wind and sun, when she came across a crumpled beer can. Normally, garbage on the beach really upset her, and she could fly into a rage at people's thoughtlessness. Today, however, she had been feeling her heart as she walked in time with her breath, and as she spied the beer can, she was struck by how the rumpled aluminum surface reflected light so beautifully. As she rotated the can with her foot to see more of the sun's reflections on the sand, a small crab scurried out of it. She felt immediately that the can was probably filled with many small beings, including organisms too small to see, a breeding ground for life on many levels. She wondered how this can must feel, having been extracted from the earth, smelted in a furnace, decorated brightly, filled with fresh beer, enjoyed by a customer, discarded, picked up by the waves and tossed about on the shore of a vast ocean, partially filled with sand and then inhabited. She felt so appreciative for the can and the experiences it gave her about the varieties of beauty. She picked up her treasure and carried it to the trash container that had many similar objects, without cursing the one who had left it for her to find.

George was casually reading the newspaper when he was drawn into an article on the condition of women in Afghanistan. Under the Taliban, a woman who had no male to accompany her could not leave her home. The severe restrictions isolated women, removing them from social contact, education and occupation; even women who were doctors could not work in the hospitals without a male escort. This was leading to widespread and deep despair; women would lie in their homes, refusing food or water, until they died. George was profoundly affected by this story, his heart physically ached. He was puzzled, since he had no connection to women in that distant country and culture. Women he knew and shared the story with were appalled, but they couldn't understand why he would be so empathetic. He asked his Heart Rhythm coach about the intensity of his emotion over the plight of others, saying, "Why does my heart feel so much?" His coach said, "That's the heart's function. Would you rather have it be numb like a stone?"

George came to understand that every heart feels what all other hearts feel, all the time, either consciously or unconsciously. His conscious experience, uncomfortable while it lasted, was still better than the vague sense of discomfort that he used to have that would lead him to self-destructive behaviors like smoking or drinking heavily, in unconscious replay of the suicidal feelings of others far away who were tugging the strings of the heart of humanity.

Depth, #7

> Don't avoid emotional pain; instead, experience your heart's pain with all your awareness, until it becomes a physical sensation. Go so deeply into pain that it becomes the pain of humanity. Let the pain turn to joy, to all feeling.

Your emotional pain may show up as physical pain; the physical pain you're aware of may be a cover over your emotional pain. When you know what causes your emotional distress, you're fortunate -- you have something to work with, although you still have to follow the emotion deeper into your heart to find its origin. This Exercise for Life is for the times when you feel upset or depressed, but you don't know exactly what you feel or why. Depression is often the result of an emotion whose validity has been denied. It is helpful to drive your emotional pain out into your body, where your physical sensations can help bring it to awareness. When your pain reaches a threshold level, it will suddenly release its message into your mind. Having broken through into conscious awareness, the pain will then subside, since its only purpose was to deliver a message from your heart.

This method of working is used by massage therapists, who delight in finding a spot that holds physical pain. An emotion can be held in your physical body, especially in a muscle, but also in skin (eczema), nasal passages (allergies), intestines (colitis), and even in bones (back ache). Rubbing that spot will make it more painful, but if the emotion can be transferred from the body to the mind, and if the conscious awareness leads to emotional healing, then the body can be relieved of it.

The heart longs to tell its story, but it doesn't speak in words; it speaks in coded languages. The location of a physical symptom is an indication of the kind of emotion behind it. Those who have no fear of the depths of their hearts can gain invaluable insights by using the physical sensations of pain as part of the language of their hearts. Heart Rhythm Meditation places great trust in the heart. While other methods seek to rise above the physical and emotional pain, we respect the sensation of pain as an urgent signal for attention to the heart. There may be physical pains that are not related to emotions, such as a cut in your finger, but most of the pains we are familiar with, such as migraines, back aches, muscle cramps, stomach aches, arthritis, neck pains, etc. contain emotional messages. They are the heart's way of getting our attention when other methods have failed. Pain breaks through our awareness like nothing else. However, we misinterpret the message, thinking the body is speaking for itself rather than as an instrument for the heart. Pain killer and mood enhancer pills simply override these important messages so that we can continue on in ignorance of our emotional condition.

Janet had a series of problems, including a financial crisis and a shaky marriage. She knew she was "down," but she didn't think she had a serious emotional condition. Every problem had its own reason, she said, and none of the reasons had to do with her emotional state. In Heart Rhythm Meditation, she was instructed to try to find her pulse in all parts of her body. She could do that easily, everywhere except in her abdomen. Below the ribcage and above the groin she could not feel any pulse. When people have not practiced Heart Rhythm Meditation, we don't expect them to be able to find their pulse anywhere, but once this inner sensation is developed, the loss of it in some area is a danger sign.

After a concerted effort, she began to feel something in her abdomen: not a pulse, but pain! This made it clear that her absence of feeling there was a defense mechanism, which then explained why she had developed a substantial belly: fat is desensitizing. The pain only appeared during meditations and disappeared afterward, meaning that the pain was an emotional signal rather than a more advanced emotional condition that had become a disease. Physical diseases need to be attended to by a physical specialist, but with Heart Rhythm Meditation the emotional cause can be discovered and treated before it creates disease.

The pain signal was shocking, but still didn't contain enough information to identify the problem in her heart. She was instructed to breathe down into the depth of her emotional heart and the depth of her torso, according to what made the pain signal more intense. In our experience, it never becomes unbearable; it is, after all, just a signal to guide our attention to the most tender spot in our physical/emotional body. Then the answer came! The pain became a clear image, with the power of a spiritual revelation at a burning bush. She was following the wrong direction in her life, working against her heart's wish and her deepest feelings. She had "swallowed" the idea that she had to do what she was doing in her career, in spite of her feeling that it was not worthy of her. It hadn't even been a conscious decision; she had followed a non-decision, and she felt stuck with it, or it was stuck in her.

Greg came to his Heart Rhythm Meditation teacher with a pain in the front of his left shoulder. He had been to a doctor and a masseuse without relief. His teacher tried a different approach: instead of relieving the pain, he would ask Greg to make it stronger. "How can I do that?" asked Greg. "By breathing through your shoulder," the teacher said. When Greg tried the technique, his breath brought his full awareness to the painful area, and it did indeed feel worse. "That hurts a a lot; how much longer do I have to do this?" asked Greg. "Until the pain speaks to you," said the teacher.

After a few more minutes, Greg could feel that the pain in his shoulder was connected to a line of pain that ran over the shoulder, down his back, to the middle of his back. "Now we're getting somewhere," said the teacher, "Just a little while longer." Greg was very uncomfortable now, struggling to breathe as the pain felt like a knife. His teacher instructed him to follow the line of pain and bring all his attention to his chest. Greg could feel the pain in his heart throb with his every heartbeat. Sweat was forming on his forehead; his hand instinctively went to his chest; his head bowed forward, and suddenly he cried out, "My mother is coming to visit me in three days!"

Greg was expecting his mother to be very critical of where he was living, and was reacting emotionally. Because he loved his mother, he refused to recognize such a reaction, and so he drove the feeling from his mind into his body. The heart always finds a way to express itself. The fact that his left shoulder was in pain had alerted the teacher to the probability that it was due to an influence he was receiving.

Karl's sister died when they were children, and his mother had died two years ago. Karl was 32 years old and longed for a loving relationship so he could settle down and raise a family. He was an attractive guy and had a decent salary as a marketing agent, but he was sure there was no one for him in the world and had considered applying to a dating service. One evening he met an old friend for a beer. The friend had been supportive of Karl for a long time, and had heard the story about there being no one for him more than once. The friend pointed out that Karl perhaps was angry at his sister and mother for leaving him alone. Karl began to realize that he had totally ignored the effect of the loss of the females in his life and how abandoned he felt because of it.

Because he trusted his friend's suggestion, he began seeing a Heart Rhythm teacher. The teacher assigned a practice of magnifying his emotions in order to experience them physically and process them emotionally in his heart. Karl took time off from work to complete this, and when he returned to work he noticed that there were a number of women who were eager to go out with him. They had been there all along, but he had not been aware of them because he was trying to avoid his emotional pain.

Depth, #8

> Forget the errors of others. Your reproach may make them more resolved in their faults. Do not dwell on your own errors either. People are seldom improved by guilt. Blame no one for anything. Rather, try to understand their reason.

We naturally feel that it is a great benefit to others to point out to them their shortcomings. In this we assume that if the other person were aware of their flaw, as obviously they are not, they would immediately take steps to correct it. But people are not so unaware as we may think, and they work on their problems more than we know. Certainly one can benefit from feedback, but criticism closes the doors of one's heart and nothing is taken in after that. When we consider how we would like to be treated by others, we see that blame does not often open us to change, but instead leads us to defend our behavior.

One of the great milestones on the spiritual path is the attainment of blamelessness: that you do not blame anyone for anything. People generally think that being blame-free is to be free of any flaw that others could blame, whereas it actually means that one's heart is in that condition of deep compassion from which no blame arises towards others. In the development of the depth of the heart, we do not expect to be free of faults; we want to be very aware of our shortcomings. We only hope to be so attentive to our own correction that we have no time for, nor interest in, correcting others.

Hazrat Inayat Khan gave this advice to those he was training to become teachers:

> When the teacher finds that the student is wrong he will not tell him that he is wrong, but will show him what is right. If the student is awakened enough to realize the difference by comparison he will be helped, and if he cannot realize it he is not ready for that conception which the teacher thinks right. Right and wrong are after all only comparative terms; in point of fact all is right and all is wrong.

He taught that a teacher should look upon their students as if looking in a mirror, seeing the faults of their students as their own faults. "In this way they can do much more for their students than anyone else in the world."

George Washington wrote 110 Rules of Civility & Decent Behavior In Company and Conversation. His 13ᵗʰ rule advises that if you see spittle on the floor in a friend's home, "put your foot dexterously upon it" to hide it, even from your host.[23] The same sentiment was expressed by Pir Vilayat Inayat Khan when he said, "Guard carefully the pride of others."

Nancy's daughter, Leyla, committed suicide when she was 45 years old. It was very hard for Nancy to go to her daughter's funeral and for years afterwards she suffered guilt and blame, trying to figure out what she had done wrong that might have caused her daughter to take her life. After practicing Heart Rhythm Meditation, Nancy had a dream one night: Leyla was in her bedroom sleeping and Nancy went to wake her as she always had when Leyla was a child. Leyla said to her: "Mom, I am healed again, and I am with you wherever you are. You can reach me in your heart anytime, just listen." Nancy awoke suddenly, sweating with the intensity of an experience she knew was real. The surprising revelation Nancy received was a great relief for her and deeply healing. She became more peaceful and accepting from this experience of the one reality she had received through Leyla. Her judgment of Leyla's action of taking her life vanished. Through her own heart opening she could experience the complexity of Leyla's emotions and events in her life that were beyond her control.

---

23 Washington's rules are based on a set of principles composed by Jesuit priests in the late 16th century. They can be found at http://www.foundationsmag.com/civility.html.

Chapter 6

Raising the Height of the Heart

6. Raising the Height of the Heart

Figure 26: Raising the Height of the Heart

This Chapter

The purpose of this chapter is to inspire your heart, restoring its optimism and raising its energy until it responds in joy. To do this, we present a special version of Heart Rhythm Meditation and eight Exercises for Life.

Lift Your Heart into Joy

Restoring the natural height of the heart is the key to overcoming depression. When the heart feels crushed, there is no enthusiasm, ambition, or energy for exploring and developing life. But the converse is also true: when there is no energy in the heart, the heart collapses. Thus the crushed condition can be reversed by introducing energy into the heart again, which we will do by breathing in a way that is is full, deep, and rich.

Energy loves to rise like smoke up a chimney, and so with abundant energy, the energetic-emotional heart is lifted. This causes every other kind of lifting: the corners of the mouth lift in happiness; the eyebrows lift in awe and wonder; the eyes lift to the vision of idealism; the chest lifts upward in pride and confidence; the hand lifts to volunteer in joyful celebration of a great cause.

Using Heart Rhythm Meditation

Full Breath

Our task is to overcome the shallow pattern of breath that is extremely common and that robs people of their strength, vitality, inspiration and creativity. A person's breath is usually shallow, with a large reservoir of air carried over from breath-to-breath. This reservoir of unexpelled air represents that part of us that we do not allow to change. Your breath is your fundamental interaction with the world, sending out the contents of your lungs and taking in the environment around us into our very cells. To be fully involved with life, we need to have a full breath. It takes effort at first because it is counter to our habit.[24]

The first reason for learning to get a full breath is that we need the energy of the inhalation to change our con- sciousness -- to become aware of what one cannot normally be aware of, to stay alert and not get sleepy, and to restore our optimism and idealism. The second reason is that it's the end of the exhalation that carries the energy of our hearts into our

---

24 See also Bair (1998), Chapter 6.

environment. (More about that in the next chapter, the Forward Dimension.)

The Rising Breath

The Rising Breath raises the height of the heart through the effect of breath.

Eight Steps

Here are the eight steps, the first five of which are the same as the Widening Breath, from Chapter four.

1. Take a majestic posture.

2. Breathe in and out through your mouth, with your lips just barely parted, sipping breath. This way of breathing gives the feeling of being free from all constraints.

3. Find your pulse. When you look for it, your pulse will appear spontaneously somewhere in your body. (The place it first appears has meaning. Can you decode the meaning from the location, given what you now know about the left and right sides of the heart and the energy centers of the body?)

4. When you finish your in-breath, hold your breath for ten seconds or so and you may feel your heart throbbing in your chest.

5. Once you can feel either your pulse or your heartbeat, use that as a counting rhythm. If you still can't feel either pulse or heartbeat, then just count mentally, slowly. You will feel the pulse eventually. Count six heartbeats while breathing out and again six heartbeats while breathing in. If that's too fast, make it eight heartbeats. Don't hold your breath at all. Using your pulse or heartbeat as a rhythm links your breath rate to your heart rate and makes the inhale and exhale the same length. Be-

cause of the periodic, balanced rhythm of the Widening Breath, we also call it the "Rhythmic Breath."

6. Extend the exhalation to increase the amount of breath you exchange in each breath cycle. As you approach the last few counts of your exhalation, squeeze your abdominal muscles to force the last bit of air out of your lungs. It takes an effort of the abdominal muscles to finish the exhalation; the diaphragm alone is not enough. Your stomach area should cave in as you breathe out. Then go immediately into the inhalation without pausing -- simply relax your muscles and new breath will rush in. You'll get at least twice as much breath per cycle by breathing this way.

7. Think of your breath as rising as you breathe in and descending as you breathe out, all the while within your heart. Your exhalation takes you deep into your heart and your inhalation lifts you high again. Ride on the breath, feeling that your breath is moving you rather than you are moving your breath.

8. As you rise in the inhalation, look for an emotion leaping out of the depth of your heart and carrying you into the heights of joy. This is glorification, an emotion of the universe that cannot be confined to a human heart. In this emotion, you can see what cannot be seen from the flatlands; you can remember the possibilities of your soul that have been covered by compromises. It's just like lifting above the fog into the clear light.

Notes on the Rising Breath

If you aren't getting a rush of energy at the beginning of your in-breath, then you're not breathing **out** far enough. Being aware of your breathing cycle, when you get to the end of your normal exhalation, breathe out for about three seconds longer. In those three seconds, empty your lungs by squeezing your abdominal muscles.

Breathe out first by relaxing your chest, then by squeezing your diaphragm muscle.

When the exhalation is full, the inhalation starts from a very deep place. It will start with a surge of breath coming in, then less and less breath comes in per second as the inhalation proceeds. To accommodate all that breath, your stomach area should balloon **out** as you breathe **in**. (Loosen your belt.) Think of the in-breath as a rising energy.

You will need to intervene at the end of the inhalation too. It's an easier intervention than you made at the end of the exhalation, which required a squeeze of the diaphragm muscles. This intervention is to expand your chest as you continue breathing in until you feel completely full of breath.

Breathe in first by relaxing your diaphragm, allowing your belly to extend out like a balloon that fills with air. Towards the end of your in-breath, expand your chest outward.

Using your heartbeat or pulse as your counter, make your Rising Breath absolutely rhythmic, the same number of beats in as out. Your breath on both inhalation and exhalation should be smooth and silent. Any noise indicates a restriction you are imposing in the flow of breath.

You could start with six heartbeats for each in-breath and six heartbeats for each out-breath. This gives a breath length of 12 seconds if your heartbeat is 60 beats per minute, or 9 seconds if your heartbeat is 80 beats per minute. You will be taking 5 to 7 breaths per minute, depending on your heart rate. When you can do 10 breaths in a row at the count of 6 heartbeats in and out, you should then slow your breath to 8 counts. If you find you can't maintain a 6 count, then you're not breathing all the way out. Try to breathe out more force fully to empty your lungs. Don't use a count below 6, to avoid hyperventilation. The Full Breath is invigorating and inspiring, but too much oxygen makes one dizzy. The solution is to breathe fully, and use a long breath. A count of at least six heartbeats in and six heartbeats out will ensure that you receive benefit from the Full Breath, and no harm.

Research has shown that if the breath rate is slowed even slightly, to 10 breaths per minute, one's blood pressure is reduced up to 36 points systolic and 20 points diastolic. Average reductions in seven clinical tests were 14/8 points.[25]

The link between breathing and blood pressure is so well understood, there is a device called "RESPeRATE" which helps those with hypertension slow their breathing. (Some of the studies cited above use this device.) Of course, why would you rely on an external device when you can re-pattern your breathing yourself?

No research has yet been performed at a breath rate of four complete breaths per minute, nor has research been done specifically on the method of Heart Rhythm Meditation, though Grossman et al. (2001) use a breathing method that slows the breath to 6 breaths per minute. Our anecdotal experience is that the sense of calm well-being that comes from breathing consciously, rhythmically and slowly produces a significant reduction in blood pressure.

---

25 Joseph et al. (2005), Grossman et al. (2001), Schein et al. (2001), Rosenthal et al. (2001), Meles et al. (2004), Elliott, White et al. (2004), Viskoper et al. (2003), Elliot, Black et al. (2004), Parati and Gavish (2003)

Exercises for Life

These Exercises for Life are designed for energizing the heart in the height dimension.

Height, #1

> Optimism is your natural condition; optimism comes from love. Consider pessimism to be a warning sign of a weakened heart.

Everyone would like to be optimistic, for optimists are happier both alone and with others than pessimists are. Optimists enjoy life more, draw others to themselves, recover from loss or illness quickly, learn and adapt rapidly, and look forward to new experiences. If it would work to say, "Don't be pessimistic; be optimistic!" then we'd say it. But it can't be done by willpower alone; the heart must power it. If your heart leaks, then the energy of the heart, which is love, will drain away and with your deflated heart you will have no choice but to be pessimistic.

When you notice any of the many versions of pessimism arising in your thoughts or being expressed in your words or actions, consider it as a warning signal that your heart is losing the energy that lifts its height. Pessimism should be your alert to act quickly to preserve your heart's nature by engaging in these exercises that raise the heart.

Here are some pessimistic phrases: "Nothing I do makes any difference"; "Avoid strangers"; "I don't feel like getting up in the morning"; "He'll never change"; "Things just keep getting worse"; "I just can't understand it"; "I could never do something great like that"; "I'm surrounded by idiots"; or "My friends will let me down".

Optimism has a price, possible disappointment, but pessimism has a greater price. An optimist takes the chance of losing; a pessimist loses the chance of gaining.[26]

Height, #2

> Regret is a waste of energy. The past has given you the present that will be opened in the future. Be resigned to the past, attentive to the present and hopeful for the future.

Wisdom is the exercise of learning from life, and there are valuable lessons in the mistakes of the past. If we do not learn those lessons, we will repeat them. But regret is not the best emotional state for learning; grateful acceptance is. When we accept our past with gratefulness for the present to which it has brought us, then we are prepared to value the lessons that life has presented.

Think of the events of the past as the sights, sounds and bumps of a taxi ride through life. When the driver stops and opens the door in the present moment, you find out where you've arrived. You had given no address, just some vague directions gathered from your life-long desires. This place may not look like what you expected, but for all you know, it might be very close to your desired destination. This present moment needs to be explored; the more you look, the more you'll find in it. When you realize the beauty of the present, how can you blame the taxi-driver for the affronts of the journey that

---

26 www.hazrat-inayat-khan.org: Message: Complete Works: Sayings: Vadan: Nirtan

brought you here? Especially when you discover that the circumstances of your present life, with all its baggage, together
with the tools you're learning to use, are a perfect preparation
for the next stage of the journey.

We seldom consider the value of the preparation that
life has made for our future. When the butterfly awakens, it
discovers its wings are stuck in the sticky cocoon of its past
life. Its struggle to free itself is an exercise that develops the
muscle strength to fly into the future. Like the butterfly, we are
struggling now in the sticky threads of our past. Will we lapse
back into what we were or leap forward into what we will
become. You determine your future by how you struggle in the
present with the consequences of your past and your future
intentions. The present you have been given is a challenge, a
puzzle, a gift and a blessing. It contains all you need to make
your next step.

You may have taken some steps downward to get here;
the path may turn upward soon. If your path has been difficult,
perhaps it's because you found a short cut. You cannot change
the past, put the present is in your hands now, and by your
attention to it and your wish for it, you are shaping the present
into the future.

*I came as I was made to come; I live as life allows me
to live; but I will be what I wish to be.*[27]

When her husband's company relocated, Janice
and her husband moved from their New England
home of twenty years, in which they had raised all
their children and where they had many friends, to a
small town in the south. She was initially caught up in

---

27 www.hazrat-inayat-khan.org: Message: Complete Works: Sayings: Nirtan: Gamakas

all the activities of the move, packing and unpacking, but as she settled down to life in a new place, she realized how much she missed her friends, her garden, and the trees, streets and shops of her old neighborhood. Her new home was too hot, her neighbors were too different in their thinking and she was isolated.

She complained as a victim of corporate policy, but she knew there had been no choice. She decided that complaining was too easy and made her too miserable. She wanted to see the change in her life as positive, but in comparison with the past, the present looked like a punishment.

The breakthrough for Janice was realizing that the present looked much better if she just appreciated it the way it is. She had moved many times before in her life, especially when she was young, she just hadn't ever moved away from a place she liked so much. This new home wasn't so bad if she didn't compare it to the place she had to leave.

Once she came to value the present, she could see it as a step in a path of many steps. This is not the end of the road, it is merely a way-station. Having moved away from a place she thought she would never leave, she felt free to move anywhere now. She could consider, "Where in the country would I like to live?" Being attentive to the present, she could be hopeful for the next step in the journey, when she and her husband would move again.

One of the key aspects of optimism is the conviction that the future will be better than the past. This is the path of the heart; apply that optimism to yourself. You are becoming a greater person, more heart-centered, able to feel the condition of others as if they are a part of yourself, and also radiating love as light into the lives of others. There may be times when you do not feel capable of these acts of the heart. In those moments your optimism is tested. Even if you do not see such qualities in yourself, you can still call upon them.

> *Assume a virtue, if you have it not.*
> *-- William Shakespeare[28]*

Height, #3

> Pursue happiness, not only pleasure. Make time for the important, not only the urgent.

What gives you pleasure may be different from what makes you happy. Pleasure is an immediate sensation that is dependent on some event; happiness is a state that builds over the long-term and is independent of any specific stimulus. The person who is happy cannot tell you why they are happy; if pressed they will speak of many things. But a person who is displeased can tell you immediately and specifically what has displeased them.

In the pursuit of happiness, you may try many amusements and vacations that take your thoughts away from the responsibilities and worries of life and give you a moment's consolation. At first it will seem that these are the moments of happiness. But these moments cannot be held, and so what seemed to be happiness will dissolve and reveal itself to be a pleasurable escape from life, instead of a happiness that can be sustained through life.

It takes insight into yourself to know what gives you happiness. There is a kind of happiness that is appropriate for each of the heart's dimensions. The deep hearts find happiness in sincerity and deep connection to a few friends; the wide

---

28 William Shakespeare, Hamlet, Act III, Scene IV.

hearts find happiness in harmonizing with many. The forward dimension of the heart drives one to happiness through activity, whereas the elevated heart is happy when aspiring to a great ideal. The full heart is happy alone; nothing is needed.

One of the ways a heart can be crushed is through an excess of busy, urgent, but unimportant transactions. Even the most capable worker can be buried by tasks to the point of failure. It is especially necessary for those with natural idealism, the characteristic of the height of the heart, to find meaning and value in their work. They would rather be idle than busy doing something that doesn't appeal to them or doesn't require their skill. To raise the height of your heart, be sure to include that work of which you can be proud and which makes a real contribution to others. High-value will lift you out of the rut of high-pressure.

Kevin's wife asked him, "Do you enjoy the feeling you get in Heart Rhythm Meditation?" "Yes, I do, very much," he replied. "And does your day go better when you meditate in the morning?" "Yes," he replied, "it generally does. Sometimes the difference is quite dramatic." "So then why don't you meditate anymore?" He answered, "I don't have time."

This conversation is quite typical, and it hides an issue of pleasure versus happiness. While our happiness depends on the healing of our hearts and restoring optimism, the process required can be unpleasant at times. First, Heart Rhythm Meditation will expose your heart's idealism, and that will contrast with your life's reality unfavorably. While you might have forgotten consciously the great wish of your heart and buried it under compromises and excuses, your heart still remembers what you have aspired to all your life. In Heart Rhythm Meditation, you will be reminded anew of what your heart has not forgotten. Secondly, your heart contains wounds that have been stored away for healing at some later time when you have developed the insight and power necessary to do it. Heart Rhythm Meditation provides that insight and power, so the wounds of the past come forward to be healed. With a brief exposure to the sun-like power of the heart, the wounds are healed and release joy, but that brief period can be painful.

Height, #4

> Hold fast to your high regard for others; don't let their weaknesses lower your opinion of them. Look for the best in people and they will come up to your estimation of them.

People are often pessimistic. If you tell them about the good in someone, they can't believe it. But if you tell them the bad of a person, they say, "Yes, that's really true."

The story of Father Flanagan and Boy's Town is the classic story about someone coming up to your vision of them. It bears repeating:

Father Flanagan insisted that there were no "bad" boys, only good boys who behaved badly. One of the boys was determined to prove him wrong, and he deliberately overturned the soup kettle in the kitchen, saying "See, Father, I am a bad boy." But Father Flanagan still replied, "I don't see a bad boy, but a lot of your friends will miss their dinner tonight." Faced with the priest's unrelenting and loving vision of him, the boy broke down and vowed to become as Father Flanagan saw him to be.

The same phenomena operates in regular life.

Barbara and John worked in the same department and often ate lunch together. Over the years, they became good friends and Barbara began to disclose her fears and difficulties to John. John was consistently positive about her, no matter what she revealed. Barbara had never had such a friendship in her life; she fully expected that John would reject her once he understood the extent of her mental problems. As John continued to be accepting and positive toward Barbara, she asked for more of his time and as he listened to her so well, she revealed more and more about her emotional world and discussed her problems with money, sexuality and her fiancee. Although Barbara was increasingly exposing her anxieties and fears, John maintained an optimistic attitude toward her problems. He said, "These things can be handled, I've had worse problems. You're a smart woman, you can make life work for you." John derived his optimistic view of Barbara from practicing Heart Rhythm Meditation, by which he had gained the insight and emotional strength to resolve his own dilemmas. Barbara never did try Heart Rhythm, but she was able through John's encouragement and faith in her to marry her fiancee, have a child and advance her career. She said, "If John had bought the view I had of myself, I would have been lost."

Puran: "When I met my meditation teacher, I was very unhappy with myself. I was keenly aware of my many problems and therapy was opening more problems with every session. I didn't know how to find the help I needed. In this extremely negative period, I met my teacher. I was impressed by the insight he had with people -- I was convinced he could see right through me. Yet he seemed to like me. This was amazing to me, that someone could see me completely and still find me likable. I was determined to learn how to see myself the way he saw me. It worked; I took the image he had of me and made it my own."

Height, #5

> Take the worst part of something and transform it so it becomes the best part, whether you are renovating your business, home or personality.

There are many improvements calling for our attention. There's the waistline, the wrinkles, and the wardrobe. There's the closet, the basement and the backyard. Then there's the need for education, counseling and spiritual growth. Personally, should you work on your inability to make new friends, tendency to be sarcastic, or lack of time management? We recommend you tackle the worst item, the one that irritates you the most. This is where you'll get the biggest reward for your effort, and the most collateral effect on the other items.

The house needed painting; the driveway needed to be resurfaced. There was rot in the bottom of the posts around the front door, and the garage door didn't close all the way. But there was one place in the house that was really embarrassing: the first-floor bathroom. Everyone avoided it, unless absolutely necessary. The wooden floor couldn't be cleaned, the shower couldn't be used and the mirror couldn't be seen in the dim light. The room had received no attention since the house was bought; there was no use painting or decorating it when the basic features of the room were dysfunctional. So that's where Mary and Tyler decided to put their attention. With tile floor, new shower and lighting, built-in cabinets, paint and paintings, the guest bath became a work of art, the pride of the house.

Sylvia had an eating disorder, a job she hated and a relationship that was failing. She was double her ideal weight, which was causing a host of other health problems that she was attempting to treat with a variety of medications. Her job kept her too busy for too little pay. Her exhaustion at the end of the day left no inspiration for her painting, the love of her soul. Her husband seemed distant to her and she craved his warmth and loving attention. Where to begin? She felt her weight problem was the most difficult for her, so her Heart Rhythm coach started there. It was indeed a difficult problem for Sylvia, whose weight was increasing monthly, not decreasing. Her recreational eating was compensating for the lack of meaning in her job and the lack of closeness in her marriage, so it seemed to be a symptom rather than a cause of her distress. But the heart's point-of-view is that every aspect of life is interconnected, serving as both a cause and an effect at the same time.

The problem of one's life can be approached from any angle; success comes not from finding the right angle but from the depth one can reach in that direction. The weight, the job and the relationship are all access points into the heart, and none of them are more causal than another. Changing any of these will change all the others. And there is an emotional cause in her heart behind all that appears.

Among the many things Sylvia told her coach, one message stood out: Sylvia said, "I feel invisible." To a coach in Heart Rhythm Meditation, that is a description of the condition of her spiritual heart, rather than her emotional or physical heart. The heart doesn't want to be invisible -- it is radiant by nature. Practicing Heart Rhythm Meditation can bring out that radiance.

There is typically a spiritual issue behind the psycho-logical issue that appears as a physical issue, such as obesity. It's the height of the heart that allows us to recognize these levels of causality, and direct our attention to the root issue.

This exercise of making the worst into the best is not only a method for efficient resource planning, it is a method for developing the height dimension of your heart. When you evaluate things in terms of "worst" and "best," you are calling upon your sense of the ideal, and this stretches your heart. The usual method of random, incremental improvements neither calls upon your heart's quality nor enhances it. Transformation is qualitatively different from improvement, and the elevated heart has no time for incremental steps -- it wants to leap!

Height, #6

> Uphold your honor at any cost. Hold your ideal high in all circumstances. You may fail to live up to your ideal, but never lower your ideal to the height of your ability.

Your ideal is supposed to be high, like a beacon the ship sees in the night, preventing it from hitting the rocks. Cynics will call your ideal "unrealistic," "naive," or even "fantastic," but an ideal is not the same as a goal; an ideal is a marker on the horizon that guides you in its direction. As the horizon recedes as you approach it, so your ideal will grow with your experience. If you accomplish your ideal, your ideal was too limited.

Sam was an executive for New-Cola, dedicated to stealing market share from Old-Cola. The Cola Wars, as they are known to insiders, are serious business that consume many lives on both sides. Those with forward energy in their hearts thrive on the competition. Those with broad hearts enjoy the community that each company offers. Those with deep hearts have found a few good friends with whom they have become close and sympathetic over many years of working together. But those who have height in their hearts struggle with the social responsibility of selling caffeinated sugar water to an increasingly stressed and overweight public. Whereas others can accept compromise more easily, Sam felt personally devalued and unable to breathe.

Sam knew he had to find a product he could believe in and he knew there were others at New-Cola that felt the same. He proposed and led the acquisition of a large orange juice company that brought a nutritious, natural beverage to the product line. That work satisfied his need for a meaningful contribution: the enormous marketing and distribution muscle of New-Cola would result in a high-quality drink being more available to more people.

Remember that your ideals are for you; others have their own ideals that are appropriate for them. There is no need to raise your ideals, unless you're working on elevating the height dimension of your heart. Your friends may be working on developing other dimensions of their hearts, so what is wrong for you may be right for them, and vice-versa.

Scott was presented with an opportunity to buy an apartment building and rent out the apartments for more than the mortgage and maintenance costs. It seemed like a no-brainer for his friend, but Scott turned him down. Scott was uncomfortable taking money from someone who was renting just because he didn't have access to the credit necessary to buy, as Scott did. "I remember when I had to rent," Scott said, "and I felt it was unfair for my landlord to build equity with my money." His friend couldn't understand Scott's "idealism;" he considered it to be stupidity. After all, renting homes was perfectly legal and very common, at least for the wealthy. But Scott wouldn't do it, on principle. "Let someone do it who doesn't see it the way I do, I don't mind. But I'm going to make my fortune another way." His friend reminded him of the college bills he would soon face, but still Scott refused. "If I never wanted to be an absentee landlord, I'm not going to change my principles just because I need the money."

When you have high ideals you can expect to be disappointed. You will fail to reach your ideals, and their pursuit will make your life harder. You will be tempted to discard your ideals as unworkable, but you need to retain them as beacons that give your life direction. You will never come up to your ideals, but you can move in their direction. Take the advice of Jelaluddin Rumi:

> Come again, come, whoever you are,
> This caravan has no despair.
> Even though you have broken your vows, perhaps
> ten thousand times,
> Still, come again, come.

Height, #7

> Do not take advantage of a person's ignorance. Seek not pleasure through the pain of another, life through the death of another, gain through the loss of another, nor honor through the humiliation of another. Influence no one to do wrong.

This Exercise for Life is a very beautiful quotation from Hazrat Inayat Khan[29] that inspires the ideal of the elevated

---

29 www.hazrat-inayat-khan.org: Message: Complete Works: Sayings: Vadan: Alankaras

heart. Every time you decline to take something whose loss would cause pain or humiliation to another, you gain a joy that cannot be taken from you. The power of the elevated heart is thereby increased, which will lift you from your doubt and restore your optimism.

Barry was a financial planner who tried to do the best for his customers. Jay asked him to review his investments and then to recommend a mutual fund by a certain company he'd seen advertised. That company, unbeknownst to Jay, offered financial planners a substantial commission beyond what other fund companies paid. Jay asked, "Is this a good mutual fund for me," and Barry answered truthfully, "Yes, it is." "Is this a popular fund," Jay continued, and Barry said honestly, "Yes, we sell a lot of it." "What was the fund's performance over the last five years?" Barry replied "Better than average for similar funds." Jay seemed satisfied, but Barry was not. Barry knew any fund's performance seeks the mean over time, and so the return ultimately depends most on how low the fund's expenses are. With the large commission this fund paid him, Barry knew the fund's expense ratio was among the highest in the industry. Although he faced a loss of fee income, Barry felt he had to explain the concept of mean reversion and the influence of expenses on returns. He could sell the fund to those who were willing to take the risk that its above average performance would continue and would offset the fund's high expenses, but Jay didn't know enough to take that risk. Jay appreciated Barry's recommendation of another fund, and was amazed when he realized that Barry would make substantially less for it. Barry's integrity cemented Jay's relationship with him and resulted in many referrals into Jay's wealthy community.

Height, #8

> Do nothing which will make your conscience feel guilty. A clear conscience gives the strength of a lion, but a guilty conscience can turn a lion into a rabbit.

A bad conscience is what makes criminals leave clues that contribute to their capture. The sense that, "This isn't right," makes a person pause when they're trying to go forward, or proceed forward with caution when they need to be bold. The conscience is culturally dependent. In American movies, the villain never gets away -- justice is always done by the end of the last reel, and this contributes to the strong ethic of fair-play that Americans have and develop in their children. Still, the American conscience is continually developing; no one would condone having a slave now, but most people still consider it fair to take advantage of an unsuspecting buyer in sales, exploit an underpaid worker in another country, or vote for a law that promotes one's own interest at the expense of the whole.

The development of the conscience is not a rational process; it's a result of the development of height in the heart. Everyone has a conscience: there is sportsmanship among hunters; there are things that soldiers in battle won't do; there is some honor even among thieves. Yet there are those who, because of conscience, would not hunt, do battle, or steal. The degree to which the conscience is developed is an indication of the height of the heart. A highly developed conscience places more restraints on a person, as appropriate for an idealistic person. If the heart is not elevated, then one's conscience is easier to live with. This exercise challenges you to live up to your conscience, whatever it is. By this aspiration, your ideals are fed, and that will elevate your conscience further.

This exercise also teaches that the height of your heart affects the forward thrust of your heart. If you violate your conscience, then your power is diminished. If your conscience agrees with your actions then you can move forward with the courage of a lion.

It is the sense of virtue that allows the heart to feel deserving. The appeal to a higher moral authority is a powerful aid, like a hand on your back with doors opening in front of you, but this appeal is unavailable when you feel guilty.

Sue was a contract programmer, and when her son's school needed a new software system for fund raising, she offered to write it for less than the expensive, commercial package they were considering. The school administrator trusted her and approved the project. Sue delivered a working system and the administrator was happy with it, but Sue had a bad conscience about it. She knew that problems would inevitably arise with it, and there would be no corporate help-desk for the school to turn to. Furthermore, all software has errors, called "bugs," which can only be discovered by exhaustive testing, which she didn't have time to do. Finally, the software would have to be updated over time for changes in the operating system, and she could not guarantee she'd be available. What she had presented to the school as a good deal would end up being very expensive to fix, maintain and upgrade. Ultimately, it would be abandoned and then further costs for purchase and training in a new system would be incurred by the school.

The next job Sue bid on, for a commercial customer, was lost to a competitor. Mysteriously, Sue lost several more bids until she accepted a contract working in software testing. Normally, she would not consider working in software testing, a definite step down for a programmer, but she needed the money. A few months into the contract, she realized in a Heart Rhythm Meditation that her present position was connected to the work she had done for the school. She was learning about the rigors of software testing now because she hadn't considered that in her bid to the school and she hadn't been able to get any programming contracts because she felt unresolved about that work.

6. Raising the Height of the Heart

Chapter 7

Extending the Heart Forward

7. Extending the Heart Forward

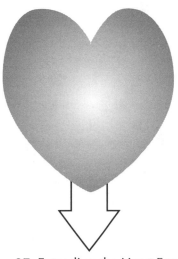

Figure 27: Extending the Heart Forward

This Chapter

This chapter is dedicated to the forward direction of the heart and to the Driving Heart that it creates. Here we will use Heart Rhythm Meditation to energize this dimension and eight more Exercises for Life to challenge and stimulate the forward direction.

Becoming Creative and Courageous

The objective in extending the heart forward is to be able to express yourself creatively and behave courageously. Becoming pushy, loud, or offensive does not show either of these strengths. The forward thrust of the heart is shown in a determined, unstoppable power that allows one to find a solution to any obstacle that may arise as one progresses in the mission of life.

Using Heart Rhythm Meditation

The Streaming Breath

Directed Breath

The ability to direct your breath through any area of your body is a natural ability, and one that mystics develop consciously. When you imagine your breath flows through your heart, you bring your awareness to your heart in a powerful way. Then your identity moves to your heart.

If you say where your center of identity is placed in your body, where would it be? In the usual consciousness, this point would be just behind your eyes, which is why we identify with our thinking. But when you breathe through your heart, that point which is the center of your self moves to the heart.

The shift in identity occurs because of a basic, innate knowledge that, fundamentally, "you" are the one who breathes. Of all the activities you can perform, it is the act of breathing that is the most essential. You can see, but you continue to exist when you can't see. You can think, but you continue to exist even when you are not thinking, as in deep sleep. Breathing is the most essential activity, and so you know the one who is breathing is your self. Now if your heart is "breathing," then "you" must be in your heart.

When you imagine your breath flows through your heart, you're visualizing the energy stream of your breath, which is separate from the air stream. The two streams, energy and air, are synchronized in time, that is, the energy stream and the air stream both flow in while you inhale, and both flow out as you exhale. You can direct your air stream through your mouth or nose, but you can direct your energy stream through any point in the body. Therefore we say you can breathe in and out of your heart because you can direct the energy stream of the breath into and out of your heart.

Eight Steps

Here are the eight steps for the Streaming Breath:

1. Sit majestically, conscious of your breath.

2. Breathe in through your mouth and out your nose.

3. Imagine your breath is coming directly out of your heart, forward, as you exhale. As you inhale, imagine your breath comes into your heart from the space in front of you, and through your ribcage.

4. Feel the pulse in your hand. (You did this before, in Chapter 3, in "Sensing the Magnetic Field by Hand.")

5. Feel your pulse in your hand and your heartbeat in your chest. Coordinate your breath with your heartbeat, six or eight heartbeats in and the same number out. (If you can't feel your heartbeat after trying, just go on to the next step.)

6. Place your palm over your heart, not touching, a few inches away from your chest. Use your hand to sense the movement of energy in and out of your chest on your breath. Imagine that the breath stream passes through your hand as a kind of transparent sensor. Can you feel a difference in sensation in your hand between your in-breath and your out-breath? Look for a subtle difference in feeling -- perhaps you'll feel your hand being pushed away from you as you breathe out, and pulled toward your chest as you breathe in. Perhaps you'll feel heat in your hand as you breathe out, and

coolness as you breathe in. If you can't feel it now, you will feel it with more practice.

This sensation of breath passing outward through your hand will convince you that your heart has a power that can carry you forward and help you accomplish your heart's wish.

7.   Now put your hand down and, breathing outward from your heart, send sunlight from your heart into the space in front of you. Your heart becomes a lamp, illuminating your path. Your heart can radiate light in this way, effort- lessly, because it is like a miniature sun.

8.   Visualize a double door in front of you. As you breathe out, imagine the doors opening out, away from you, letting your breath and influence pass into a further and greater space. As you breathe in, feel a hand upon your back, providing fresh energy and support. What your heart can accomplish now is unlimited.

Results of the Streaming Breath

There is no fear when the light from your heart pene- trates the darkness. There is no doubt or confusion in follow- ing the path that your shining heart reveals. Your mind be- comes brilliant and clear like a crystal when the light of your heart is present within it. The doors to all possibility open in front of your open heart. Hazrat Inayat Khan described the one whose heart is energized in this way:

> The clouds of doubt and fear are scattered by thy pierc- ing glance; all ignorance vanishes in thy illuminating presence. [30]

---

30 www.hazrat-inayat-khan.org: Message: Complete Works: Sayings: Vadan: Gayatri, "Pir"

Exercises for Life

Forward, #1

> Feel the wish of your heart, that which your heart has wished for all your life, and still desires.

There is a thread that runs through all the events of your life, like the cord that strings the beads in a necklace. Looking back over your life, can you see a consistent interest in some subject, kind of activity, type of person, or aspiration? This is a clue to the purpose of your life. Your purpose was engraved into your heart before conception, that you might eventually discover it there and make it your conscious wish.

Elisabeth Kübler-Ross, who worked with the dying, said that at the end of life, people often have two regrets that torment them and keep them from passing into peace. One is the regret that they have not done what they wanted to do in life, and the second is that they have not become what they wished to become.[31]

There is a wish in your heart that no one put there, and no one can remove. You can bury it under the many urgencies of life and put it out of your mind, but your heart holds it forever and presents it to you at critical junctures in your life. This wish corresponds to the unusual skills you've been given, even if you haven't discovered those skills.

For Roger, the wish had to do with music; he knew that much. He had no real training in music; during school he had been too insecure to risk embarrassment in a performance art when he could safely excel in mathematics. Music was his heart; math was

---

31 Kübler-Ross (1969)

his mind, and following his mind made more sense and led to more predictable outcomes than pursuing his heart's interest -- how would that lead to making a living?

Roger had noticed that he seemed to have an unusual ability, at least in relation to his friends, of being able to remember a song accurately. Whereas most people would change a few notes in recalling a song, he could recall a song's melody and rhythm exactly. This skill had limited usefulness in his career as a computer programmer.

After his retirement, Roger's Heart Rhythm Meditation raised his love for music as a consistent theme, so he joined a choir and found his voice. Through coaching and practice, he found he could sing as well as his uncle, whose singing skill had been legendary in his family and widely renowned. What to do with this new-found skill? Had he discovered it earlier in his life, for he now knew it was a latent ability he'd always had, he might have tried to make his living through his music. It would have become part of his identity and he would have used it to gain the respect and recognition from his peers and society that he had received instead through his computer career. Now his needs were less personal; his interests more social. Even though he had just learned how to sing, and in spite of his lack of professional training, he had come to the same sort of place he might have reached after a long career as a singer -- dedicated to using music for a purpose rather than for self-exploration.

Roger realized immediately that music was a description of the harmony that might be found between people. It gave him a language and methodology to communicate to others what he had been wanting to say about human relationships. He had been trying to help his children and a few of his friends with the relationship issues they had with their spouses and children, and now he felt he had a way to express

what he couldn't say. Roger started a kind of counseling practice where he taught couples to sing together, especially people who didn't think they could
sing. The problems they encountered in trying to harmonize together were their same old relationship
problems, now demonstrated musically. He was using
musical harmony as a metaphor for social harmony. A
new chapter of his life began, one that he could have
missed if he hadn't heard the guidance of his heart.

Forward, #2

> Become passive with respect to the power of the
> heart within you.

Your heart has its own power, and this power is the
greatest power you have. Therefore you do not need to add
anything to it. Let your heart do its own work, toward its own
desire. It will do this best if you do not get in the way by seeking diversions or engaging in self-destructive behavior.

Bob was a senior executive in an international
bank who was in a serious conflict with his boss, who
berated Bob frequently in front of the other managers
for his low profit numbers. Bob responded to this
treatment by making greater and greater efforts to ex-
ert his control over his staff, but despite his pressure,
his results worsened. Then, through Heart Rhythm
Meditation, he found a natural power in his chest,
one that didn't need to be pushed. He began to see
his staff differently than he had, and made changes in
the way he related to them.

The simplest change Bob made was to stop
threatening to fire his staff if they didn't do what he
wanted. Motivational speeches weren't what they
needed either; they needed help, and Bob became
their coach. While he had detested the threatening

and bullying that he had been prodded into, he loved helping people. His natural style of management was actually more effective for him than the carrot and stick approach of his boss. He got his numbers up, and his blood pressure down.

The heart operates like a powerful magnet, able to draw toward you those people, events and opportunities that it needs to fulfill its wish.

The heart is the actor; it uses the personality, mind and body as instruments. The whole universe responds to its wish.

Hector was a man with an unusual belief: he believed he was about to meet a woman who would be his life partner, his soul-mate. He didn't used to believe in such a mythical person, but now he had to -- she appeared in his every meditation. All through the winter and spring he had the feeling he was going to meet her at a conference he had planned to attend in the summer. He wondered how he would find her there, and would she recognize him?

When the time of the conference finally came and he arrived at the hotel, he headed first for the dining room, as he had traveled all day and was very hungry. He sat down at a table, and immediately a woman came up to him and said, "Professor Rodriguez, I'm on the conference staff; I'm supposed to greet the presenters. I've been waiting for you to arrive and I noticed you come in here. When you're through eating, just drop into the reception area and I'll help you get your badge and materials." He recognized her at once, and amazed, asked her to sit down.

As they talked together, Hector was completely convinced that she was the one he had been seeing in his Heart Rhythm Meditations. Within the hour, he had proposed to her. She was smitten by his charm but put off by his certainty. They met again and again as she realized he was sincere. By the end of the week they were spending all their free time together. But the possibility of their being together longer was very remote. She had a life, a career and a family, and he had his work in a distant city. It was as if mountains would have to be moved to make way for their love.

For three years, he held out hope for this relationship. He had no outer contact with her as she attempted to make her marriage work and became pregnant with her first child, but he had a daily inner contact through Heart Rhythm Meditation: he felt her presence. His friends ridiculed his devotion, but he persisted. He had been given the vision of her, and she had appeared just as he foresaw. Now she was a living presence in his heart; he wasn't going to give up. Finally, she called. "I'm ready to be with you now. Do you still want me?" she asked. He was not surprised; he had felt her increasing disengagement from her husband. "How soon can you come?" he replied. They've been married now for 19 years, but Hector would have missed the love of his life if he had not believed in the power of his heart.

Forward, #3

> Do something every day toward the accomplishment of your heart's wish.

Your heart's wish begins like a delicate plant -- it needs care and frequent watering. As it matures, it gets hardier, but it still needs a little fence around it for protection. Later it becomes like a tree that can stand up even to powerful winds. It sends out branches that create a micro ecosystem on which other plants, animals, birds and insects depend. Eventually it becomes a forest. The heart's wish has become your whole life.

What is needed in the beginning is consistent attention. When your attention wavers, the wish falters. When your life has taken a turn that is very different from how you'd like to live, then your heart's wish is like a seedling in the dark.

Every day your heart's wish needs to be watered by your attention. Amid all the distractions of life, you demonstrate your dedication to the accomplishment of your heart's wish by asking yourself, "What can I do today to advance toward my goal?" The best time to do this is right at the end of your morning session of Heart Rhythm Meditation, when your attention is already on your heart. The greatest difficulty in accomplishing your heart's wish is to remember it consistently; most people forget what it is they're asking for, then remember it suddenly and despair that it hasn't been accomplished yet. With Heart Rhythm Meditation, your heart will remind you in every session.

Forward, #4

> Have more effect upon the world than the world has upon you.

There is a switch in yourself that can be thrown either way: either you are more aware of what comes toward you, or more aware of what comes from you. Most people have this switch on its default setting: consider the actions that others and the whole environment have upon you, and respond to that. But the person with the extended, forward heart has more concern for their own effect upon others. In simple terms, it's "giver" or "receiver."

Puran: In the 1970's, I was part of an experiment being run by a doctor in Boston. He had a theory that meditation would allow people to quickly reduce their stress, as shown in their adrenaline level. To test this, he had to induce a standard level of stress in his subjects, then draw blood every 30 seconds for a later hormone test. He induced stress by packing the right arm in ice, from the fingertips to above the elbow. Most people's tolerance of the pain that induces is shorter than a minute.

With a syringe in one arm and the other arm in ice, I began to meditate. Spontaneously, I looked over at the ice and had the thought, "That ice is doomed; I'm going to melt it." The usual thought would have been, "My arm hurts; that ice is going to freeze it." Which will it be? It depends on which way the switch is thrown. The way you look at it is the way it goes.

If you try this experiment, you'll see that you can't just decide whether to melt the ice or be frozen by the ice. Once the pain begins, you'll find it difficult to think clearly, and the concept of a hot arm will seem very unrealistic. Your body will abandon your arm to save the rest of you. Now put your left hand on your heart and think of your breath and your heart together. This will change the energy in your body and your circulation in your arm will switch from constricting the blood flow, to increasing the blood flow. Your arm will become warmer than usual and it won't be in pain.

The key to this built-in switch that we all have is to use your heart, not your mind. When you feel wealthy, you become generous automatically. When your heart feels powerful, it becomes radiant; it creates and expresses itself. It is aware of the environment, but also of its ability to change the environment.

The deer is a very sensitive and alert animal. It sees and feels everything in its environment. If it senses that the environment is not suitable, it can flee very quickly. The beaver has a different approach; it seeks out a valley with a small stream and transforms that valley into a lake by building a dam. It can't live in the valley; it can only build its home on a lake. So it makes a lake. The beaver creates its own ecosystem; the deer must find an ecosystem it can tolerate.

The deer has a deep, sensitive heart; the beaver has a forward, creative heart. If you want to be like the beaver, you have to have the power to change your world. That power is in the forward dimension of your heart.

Forward, #5

> Consider every problem as a challenge to the power of your creativity.

When the creative solution is found, the problem's contribution to your growth will be appreciated. The result will endure and the problem that stimulated it will be forgotten.

Karen's landlord is seeking to evict her unless she pays an additional $200 per month for excessive wear and tear due to her frequent guests. Her lease specifies she can have a guest stay with her for up to 30 days, and her beautiful home and the warm California climate its in attracts her friends all year long. In the winter she's non-stop.

The landlord presents her with a simple choice: pay more rent or stop having guests. From her own point-of-view, she also sees the situation simplistically: her lease gives her the right to have guests, so she will take advantage of that right. But this does not consider the concern of the landlord and no lasting solution can ignore that.

Karen meditated with her heart and saw that her landlord wants assurances that his property is not being damaged. She saw that he's a poor judge of character, so he doesn't realize that Karen is a trustworthy tenant who is actually caring well for the property. Suddenly she saw a solution: the dining room had an inexpensive hanging light that failed to illuminate the table and she had wished for a more sophisticated light that she could raise and lower. Although this was not the provence of a tenant, she decided to buy the lamp and install it herself. She would benefit from a nicer lamp, and the landlord might be persuaded that she was someone who would take care of the place.

She installed the light and sent before-and-after pictures to the landlord. He was impressed, and stopped pressing for a rent increase.

The important part of Karen's story is not that she thought of a clever third option to what had been a black-or-white situation, but that in doing so she overcame her tendency to feel victimized by people in power, like a landlord, and helpless against their authority. Her use of Heart Rhythm Meditation unfroze her heart so she was able to act creatively.

Sam was a project manager for GE with ten years seniority, but that didn't keep him from being laid off. When it happened, it was like his world had collapsed upon him. His whole career had been at GE; he knew gas turbine engines and very little else. For six months he tried to find similar work, but there were no project management jobs of any kind. He fell into a depression and fought with his wife, who was now the sole breadwinner. She knew about the Exercises for Life and challenged him to be creative: "Even though you didn't choose this situation, you can use it to your advantage if you'll just use some creativity."

She had been doing Heart Rhythm Meditation for a few months, and shared what she knew with Sam.

While Sam was breathing through his heart, his emotions started to change from despair over the loss of his former position to relief and then to happiness about having time to do some house maintenance. As he thought about that, still breathing through his heart, he felt excited about not just repairing the cracked spot in the ceiling, but restoring the whole room to its original Victorian condition. It was like a discovery of a buried, ancient wish, in this case the wish to re-create an art form that few valued anymore.

Sam borrowed money and went to a school for restoring antique homes. Now he's a project manager again, but the projects are for his clients, who eagerly seek his services to bring to their homes the quality workmanship of an earlier age. He's discovered an ideal buried in his heart that has become his life's work, thanks to GE and his wife's encouragement.

Forward, #6

> You can have whatever your heart wants most. Indeed, the path to its attainment is already prepared for you. It is your birthright that has created your desire.

In the path of the heart, we value your heart's desires as sacred signs of the purpose of your life. You can become aware of your destiny by noticing the wishes of your heart. The nature of the heart's desire has been addressed by many teachers over the millennia. One view has been that personal desire is a product of the ego, and therefore a distraction on the path to selflessness and enlightenment. We do not hold that view.

The path of the heart honors the heart above all else. We cannot honor the heart and dishonor its function as the treasure chest holding our life's desire. As all hearts are connected and all hearts reflect the same, one heart, the desire that your heart feels is a reflection of the desire of all people everywhere. So the desire you feel is a taste of a larger desire that lives in the heart of humanity. Your consciousness of a desire arising in your heart is a signal that the desire has been prepared during the time it was unconscious and is now ready to be delivered to you. Consider it as your birthright, waiting to be claimed.

To say this again in another language, it is God's own desire that arises in your heart as your desire. To repress this desire would be to suppress a divine impulse.

The desire we speak of is not a whim of the mind. For the mind's whim, only the power of the mind is available, but for the desire of the heart, the full power of the heart is available. The heart's magnetism that draws what it desires to itself and repels all obstacles, is reserved for the heart's true desire.

Puran: When one of my sons, Ethan, was ten years old, he showed considerable interest and talent in singing and performing. In a meditation one morning in August, I discovered I had a very strong wish to have him attend The American Boychoir School in Princeton, New Jersey. I had known of the school when I was young; it teaches the boys the greatest choral music, both religious and modern, and gives them the chance to perform nationwide and abroad. I talked to Ethan about it and he was very excited.

I called the school to inquire about having Ethan start there at the beginning of the next school year, which was a month away. The head of admissions was amused: "First of all," she said, "admission is only by audition. Secondly, the school is full and there are two boys on the waiting list. Usually families plan years ahead. Thirdly, the school costs $20,000 a year," an amount that was way out-of-reach for us. I had three good reasons to consider this desire of mine futile, but I knew my desire was from my heart, so I knew there was a way already prepared to satisfy it. I asked if we could have a tour of the school anyway, and we drove six hours to Princeton the next weekend.

Walking around the campus, I had tears in my eyes. I deeply felt this was perfect for Ethan. I asked how an audition might be arranged. "They're only done by the choirmaster, usually while the choir is on tour," I was told. I asked, "By chance, is the choirmaster here at the school this weekend?" "Well, yes, he is." "So could he give Ethan an audition today?" "I'll see." It was arranged, and in a short time I was standing outside the window listening to Ethan sing a song he knew. I was elated when I saw the choirmaster coming out with his arm around Ethan. "The best audition I've given this year," he said. When the Head of Admissions asked, "If he were admitted, would Ethan definitely attend," I replied, "It is his destiny."

Ethan started at the American Boychoir three weeks later, on scholarship. He attended all four years, and was then courted by several fine private high schools. He sang through college, where he became a Cantor in the Jewish services. The Boychoir experience was indeed perfect for him, but he would have missed it had I not been sure that a way was prepared for the fulfillment of my wish, in spite of all appearances.

Forward, #7

> Do not spare yourself in the work which you must accomplish.

When you have become aware of your life's purpose, that continual wish that has permeated your whole life in various forms, and you are engaged in some activity that furthers this purpose, then how hard should you work at it? With all your heart, all your mind, and all your breath.

Imagine asking Johann Sebastian Bach, "How hard do you work on your music?" He would have said something like, "It's all I do; I do nothing else." While some may say, "It's taken over your life," he would reply, "It is my life. I give my life to music and it gives life back to me."

The sense of purpose is a deep and inherent aspect of the heart. In every heart there is a profound emotion of gratitude that life has been given to one, and an unshakeable knowledge that this gift has been for some purpose. People who are unaware of their hearts have only a faint sense of their purpose, but those who consciously engage their hearts recognize the calling, "There is something I must accomplish in my life." A contribution to life must be made to honor the gift of life we have been given. When you find that which you feel you must accomplish, then you know what life is for. Don't hold back; this is the time for action.

In the civil rights and peace movement of the 60's, we used to ask for "your money or your life." There were generous supporters of the peace movement that paid the necessary costs and put up bail money for demonstrators who were arrested. But even more valuable than money was people's time. The way people allocate their time is the true test of their priorities.

When we were doing management consulting in the 80's, Managing By Objectives (MBO) was the rage, so we wrote and used a computer program that analyzed how managers spent their time in service of their objectives. A typical manager, Katherine, had a set of objectives given to her and a few others she added to round out her job experience and prepare her for promotions. When we asked Katherine what her management objectives were, she could rattle them off in priority order, but we suspected her actual priorities were different.

This analysis involves a matrix: in the left column down the page, list all the activities you do in a week, and how long you spend on each. An activity is like having a meeting with your staff, visiting a branch office, designing a new marketing campaign, doing job performance reviews, reporting to senior management, etc. List your objectives across the top of the page as column headers. Objectives might be like increasing revenue, reducing expenses, gathering market share, improving product quality and bettering shareholder relations. Then for each activity on the left, indicate its impact to each of your management objectives on a 1-to-10 scale, putting the number in the appropriate column of the row for that activity. Now multiply the time spent on an activity times the impact it has on an objective and put that in one cell of the matrix. Repeat for all activities and objectives. Finally, add the products in each column for a total by objective. The relative values of these totals show the real priority for each objective, according to how you actually spend your time.

Every manager we did this with was surprised; some were absolutely startled. The objectives they claimed had the highest priority were not getting nearly as much attention as objectives much further down their official list. They were not spending their time on what was supposed to be important; they were giving their time away to to lesser goals.

You are a manager too, of your own life. Look at your week and how you spend your time -- this will show what's really important to you. Look at your checkbook and see how you spend your money. That will show what's valuable to you. One cannot argue with these objective measures of the resources of your life. There's no use complaining that you don't have enough time or money; for what purpose do you spend what you have?

No one is surprised at the thought that people, even highly-paid professional managers, waste large amounts of time. We all see this in our own lives. Every moment of your life on earth is precious, and every moment is spent one way or another. Giving in to diversions and worries is a kind of resistance to your purpose. You're holding yourself back, as if you're saving your energy for something else. That's OK for someone who hasn't found their purpose, but it won't do for someone who has a reason to expand their heart in the forward dimension.

Thinking that you are not worthy, worrying what others think of you, being inquisitive about the affairs of others, overindulging yourself, arguing and complaining are all a waste of time to someone who wants to energize the forward dimension. They all reduce the power of the forward thrust of the heart, a vital power that is just sufficient to accomplish what you are meant to accomplish.

Forward, #8

Once you have allowed a wish into your heart, you must accomplish it. The only exception is when you grow beyond it, like a child outgrowing his toys.

This is a very sobering thought. Just think of all the wishes you've ever had, and how many of them you've accomplished. What happens to all those unaccomplished wishes? They go "underground" into one's unconscious and contribute to a sense of pessimism and unworthiness, while they continue to activate the magnetic power of the heart.

Be careful of the claim that you've grown beyond what you haven't achieved. This is the classic "sour grapes" story, where the man who can't grasp the grapes he is stretching to reach says to himself, "They're probably sour anyway." If you want grapes, you must get them; any failure to achieve what you want is a weakness in the forward dimension of your heart, and this will lead to resentment and jealousy. If you've really grown beyond something, the one exception to this rule of attainment, then you wouldn't want the object even if it were given to you.

Susanna: I studied theater at an experimental drama school and did a few TV movies in Vienna. From this experience I realized I wanted to become a director and work with a group of women to develop an original play about the women's movement. I gathered a group in Austria and began a creative process with them, and I made some connections with women in Switzerland, Germany and England to do performances of our play there. As with so many theater groups in those days, the women's theater group fell apart after six months without developing anything. I was very disappointed, but I knew I didn't want to end my theater career this way. I had the in-tuition to go to Switzerland and bring a play to life there. I followed through with that intuition -- I packed up my belongings in my VW bug and visited Monica in Basel, my contact in Switzerland.

I found out that Monica had formed a women's theater group, and they were in need of a director. They could be accepted at the Stadtheater if they only had a director. After some introductory work with the group I made a proposal to the Stadttheater, which was accepted, and I became the director. Six months later we had a premier opening at the Kleinen Buehne of the Stadttheater, Basel. It was sold out in all five performances, and then we took it on tour to Berlin and Zurich, where all performances were sold out as well.

Years later, I'm still so glad that I pursued my dream of directing. Although I'm no longer in theater, the experience of both acting and directing continues to enrich my work as a seminar leader, and the success I had gives me confidence in my intuition, creativity and perseverance.

Janice had an uncle when she was small who had a corner office in the bank building. He was a very powerful man, obviously. She was always impressed by the wonder of his office furniture, thick carpet and fancy telephone. Janice married young and dedicated herself to raising her children instead of gaining job experience. By the time she entered business later in life, she had long given up any hope of becoming accomplished, influential and powerful like her uncle was.

She was given a small cubicle in the center of a large room, far from any windows and surrounded by similar cubicles. She said she loved her job, and she was indeed glad to have an income, but secretly she hated everything about it. The District Manager in the corner office was the one she hated most. Even to herself she could not admit that she wanted his space; that would be insolent, yet she found herself frequently walking by it. When he wasn't there, she would peer in; there was something about it that was so familiar and compelling.

In Heart Rhythm Meditation, Janice realized that her feelings for the District Manager were really jealously. She was angry at work because she felt her destiny had been denied her. She felt determined to rise to a position of power, in spite of her late start and lack of experience. Her heart, awakened to the wish it had held from an early age, responded strongly, filling her with inspiration and resolve. Her attitude changed; she began to feel as if she were already responsible for the company's success. She went to school; she immersed herself in the technology and marketing of the company's product. The company was acquired and merged twice, and she took advantage of the opportunities.

After ten years, she was one of the few left. When she was chosen to start a new department, it was she who laid out the floor plan. She smiled as she placed a conference room in her corner of the 23rd floor. It would be a beautiful space for her staff to share, and she designed a smaller but quite attractive office for herself next door. After all, the wish of her heart was for responsibility and influence rather than corner windows. She did give herself a leather chair and desk, though.

Hazrat Inayat Khan gave great emphasis to the importance of completing one's wish:

An important rule of psychology is that every motive that takes its root in the mind must be watered and reared until its full development. And if one neglects this duty, one does not only harm the motive, but by this the will power becomes less, and the working of the mind becomes disorderly. Even if the motive be small and unimportant, yet a steady pursuit after its attainment trains the mind, strengthens the will, and keeps the inner mechanism in order.

For instance, when a person tries to unravel a knot, and then he thinks, 'No use giving time to it,' he loses an opportunity of strengthening the will and attaining the object desired. However small a thing may appear to be, when once handled, one must accomplish it, not for the thing itself, but for what benefit it gives. Yes, thought must be given as to its importance and value in the beginning, when the motive begins to take root in the mind, and one must avoid an undesirable and unimportant motive taking place.

When the motive does not receive a direction, it does not necessarily die away. It takes its own path and culminates in some shape and form quite different from what you had desired. All ugliness, crookedness, and defect in nature and art is mostly caused by this.

7. Extending the Heart Forward

Chapter 8

Expanding the Inner Heart

8. Expanding the Inner Heart

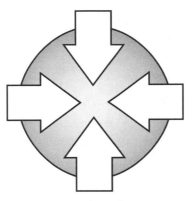

Figure 28: Expanding the Inner Heart

This Chapter

This chapter explores the inner dimension of the heart, your treasure of heart energy, ready to be drawn upon to respond to change or to be drawn out into one of the other dimensions. This inner wealth can be built up and spent down, like a bank account. However, unlike a bank account, you have to pay interest on that heart energy that you've saved up and haven't used. The heart is not a perfect container -- every heart has been wounded in life and its wounds have caused holes, like ulcers, that leak its stored energy. As long as the heart is being recharged, these leaks are not noticeable, but if the inspiration into the heart is stopped or slowed significantly, then the level of energy in the heart drops. If it drops enough, one slips from optimism into pessimism.

Recharging the Heart

As discussed earlier, in Chapter 6 and elsewhere, optimism is the natural condition of the heart; it is a condition associated with the height of the heart. Each dimension has an effect on the others; when the inner dimension is weak, all dimensions are limited. If the heart is emptied, optimism cannot be sustained, nor can empathy, tolerance, initiative, and so forth. We have all these qualities naturally, but life tests us, and the qualities can be depleted; the inner dimension of the heart replenishes the others.

Your emotional heart may also have developed deadened parts, like scar tissue in a physical heart, where the feeling is lost. These areas are hard to find because you no longer notice the absence of what you once felt, or what others still feel.

You have undoubtedly found ways to recharge your heart. What do you do when you feel depleted? Perhaps you retire to be by yourself with a good book, or walk into nature. Perhaps you seek out a friend -- the exchange of heart energy that occurs through dialogue can inspire both hearts, or drain both. Perhaps you shoot baskets, or run, or swim -- the increased exertion from exercise pumps energy into the heart. We recommend that you learn Heart Rhythm Meditation as a very efficient and effective method of recharging your heart. When your heart is energized your inner wealth is great, and your home is where your treasure is.

Using Heart Rhythm Meditation

The Expanding Breath

Here is the grand practice of coordinating the heartbeat and the breath: The Expanding Breath. The Expanding Breath brings together most of the things we've done so far: conscious breath, full exhalation, feeling the heartbeat, and breathing through the heart. Many people find that the Expanding Breath is the foundation of their practice.

The period of stillness in the breath cycle is longer than you might expect, but holding the breath is important.[32] While your breath is held in the heart, your heart is forced to expand energetically. Never pause after the exhalation, when you're out of breath; pause only when you're full of breath; breath is life. Hold that life energy in your heart and cherish it there as you feel the thumping of your heart. Then give it all away as you breathe out, and receive a new life as you breathe in again.

This form of Heart Rhythm Meditation uses a breath that has a square pattern, where the time of exhalation forms one side, as seen in Figure 29. Notice that the breath is held after the inhalation, never after the exhalation.

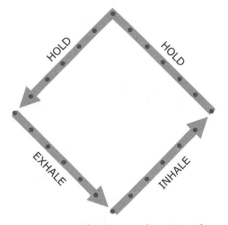

Figure 29: The Expanding Breath

The Expanding Breath is the perfect breath pattern for meditation, with equal time for experiencing the timeless held breath and the moving breath of time, an equal balance be-

---

32 Bair (1998), Chapter 7

tween in-breath and out-breath, and a guarantee of a successful, full exhalation, all the while focusing the mind on the heart.

Instruction

Start with a basic count of 6 heartbeats, making each side of the square take about 6 seconds. Breathe out for six heartbeats; breathe in for 6 heartbeats; hold your breath for 12 heartbeats. Then if that seems too short, go to 8-8-16. If too long, use 4-4-8.

By using the clock of the heartbeat, your breath will become more stable and regular than ever before. You couldn't have such a regular breath without a source of timing, and the timer we use is the most natural: the heartbeat. If your exhalation is 6 heartbeats long, then the frequency of the heartbeat becomes the 24th harmonic of the frequency of the breath. Thus the two, major, dominant organic oscillators, or clocks, of the body are synchronized together.

Difficulty in holding the breath is usually due to not breathing out enough. The principle is, the longer you breathe out, the longer you can hold your in-breath. In the Expanding Breath, where the time of the exhalation is fixed, you may have to use those last three seconds of your exhalation to expel more air than you have been.

The Expanding Breath guarantees that the exhalation is complete because if it isn't, you can't maintain a square breath pattern. If you don't reach the end of your exhalation you will run out of breath later in the cycle. Use the last heartbeats of your exhalation to squeeze your diaphragm a little more. You will likely find there was more air there, waiting to be discovered and expelled.

Be patient. This takes practice to learn. And it's surprising that it's not so hard physically or mentally, but emotionally. There is a reason why we learn to breathe shallowly: it's a defense mechanism. As you push through that last bit of held breath at the end of the exhalation, your resistance goes up quickly. It's the same feeling we get when we feel overexposed or defenseless. That last bit of breath that you hold onto is a buffer between you and the ultimate fear, the fear of death. When you release that breath, you confront your vulnerability.

By finishing you exhalation, you are building your faith. That's an amazing claim, but it's faith that allows you to go to the point of no breath, where you are then completely dependent on your next inhalation, with no reserve. This breath expresses the philosophy of the heart: give all that you possess and accept all that is given to you.

So this simple little practice, the Expanding Breath, that is so technical, is really all about your heart's condition. A pain you have in your heart, conscious or unconscious, may surface and disrupt your breath rhythm. By watching your breath, you'll observe this change and this will alert you to the emotion. Find it with thankfulness; a powerful force that has been directing your life has now become conscious. Conscious emotion can be harnessed; unconscious emotions have to act out.

Here's some tips about doing the Expanding Breath that we have learned from experience:

1. When you can't sense your heartbeat, imagine it instead and keep to your rhythm.

2. The sensation of breathing can overwhelm the sensation of your heartbeat. To make it easier to feel your heartbeat

during the in-breath and out-breath cycles, you can try breathing in short puffs in-between heartbeats. Exhale in six little puffs of air, one per heartbeat. Make a tiny pause after each puff, and in that pause you can feel your heartbeat. Inhale also in little puffs, one per heartbeat, until you reach the top of the breath. This is not ideal; the ideal is a smooth, continuous breath with awareness of each heartbeat as they occur.

3. Picture your breath pattern as a diamond-shaped pathway placed over your body and centered on your heart. Each of the four sides is equal length. The exhale starts at your left shoulder and descends on your left side; the bottom of the breath is deep in your solar plexus; the inhalation rises on the right side to your right shoulder; the breath is held through a further rise on the right side that peaks above your head and continues through a descending path to your left shoulder.

The advantage of this vision of the square, or diamond, is that circumambulation focuses energy on the center, which is the heart. Your mind traces a path around and around the heart, and that causes a vortex of attention that pulls all your mental energy into the center of the pathway, your heart.

For a few days, maybe a week, the technique will dominate the experience. There's so much to think about and there may be an anxiety of not doing it right that will make it even harder. Anxiety needs a lot of breath, so it will disrupt the rhythm. All of this is predictable, so relax.

While it is easy to get the heartbeat when you hold your in-breath, it is harder to notice it as you breathe out, and then in. But it will be there again when you hold your breath. With practice, you'll be able to feel your heartbeat throughout the breath cycle. Until you can, just count the length of your breaths in the rhythm of your heartbeat.

If you lose your heartbeat during the Expanding Breath, you can continue with your pulse. If you also lose your pulse through part of the breath cycle, you can keep the same rhythm of the name and synchronize your rhythm when you do feel it again.

In a week of practice, the Expanding Breath may become natural. When you've developed the skill of holding the square pattern for ten breaths in a row, you should celebrate! This is a major accomplishment of mastery. You've established a base camp on the mountain, a plateau from which you will begin the journey into the depths and the heights of your heart, your greatest treasure. Let yourself be moved by the beauty of its rhythm, its simple perfection, and the eternal age of its balance.

Exercises for Life

Inner, #1

> Throughout the day, keep your heart energized by touching your heart with the energy of your breath and placing your attention on your heartbeat.

Your heart is so sensitive it is easily wounded, but it also has the amazing ability to heal itself. Your heart makes its own medicine and heals its own wounds, if only you provide it with your attention and the energy of your breath. Without attention and energy, the heart's wounds will fester in one of two ways: a wound may become an ulcer which bleeds the inner energy of the heart, leaving you weak of heart and hollow, or a wound may form a scar which is a deadened part of the heart, leaving you insensitive and cold. These debilitating conditions can be healed to restore the heart's power and sensitivity, but the cure will require attention and training of your breath to carry energy.

Heart Rhythm Meditation is designed specifically to provide this attention and energy through breath that is coordinated with the heartbeat, and we do this in practice sessions, either alone or in a practice group. This Exercise for Life is a reminder that you can also energize your heart anytime -- in the midst of a crowd, in a business meeting, while talking with your children -- by simply thinking of your heart and imagining that your breath and voice come from there.

Jack had been married four times; each time, he was the one that ended the relationship. In each case he had good reasons, he told himself. But as he became attentive to his heart in Heart Rhythm Meditation, he could no longer ignore the unusual statistics: he had walked away from three women and no women had walked away from him. Somehow, he realized, he was just not sensitive to the pain of being left. If he had been sensitive to that terrible pain, he could not have inflicted it three times. Some part of his heart was deadened, like scar tissue, so he didn't feel the abandonment and betrayal he caused in his wives.

Through daily Heart Rhythm Meditation, his heart received what it needed to heal itself, and he discovered one day, quite suddenly, what was the scar in his heart. His father had left when he was small, and Jack had survived the loss, but he had deadened that part of his heart that felt what it was like to be left. As a young child, he had unconsciously decided to never feel that again -- it was too horrible. It was his insensitivity to this kind of pain that allowed him to leave others.

After Jack's scar was found, the solution developed. The experience of being left had to come alive again, as it was before it was buried. Though Jack couldn't go back to a child's experience of being abandoned by a man he never saw again, he could find this emotion in the present, in his relationship with his Heart. There he could feel the longing for closeness and the anguish of distance, the despair of feeling guilt for being left and the utter confusion of trying to understand why. He asked his Heart, "Am I not worthy of being held in Your Presence and feeling Your Love all around me? What have I done to alienate You from myself? Why won't you be tangible and visible in my life?" And he recognized that his ex-wives all had felt something like that when he left them, even though they had done nothing wrong.

With the intense energy and attention that Heart Rhythm Meditation focused on his heart, Jack's heart began to heal its scar. Being able to feel loss gave him the ability to feel closeness.

Then Jack became aware of a second kind of wound in his emotional heart: an ulcer that leaked his heart's energy. This wound was also connected to his father's abandonment of the family, making Jack totally dependent on his mother. While Jack had become insensitive to the loss of his father, he was hyper-sensitive to the attention of his mother. He did everything he could to make her happy with him and if he ever displeased her, he turned into emotional jelly: all his strength drained out of him and he could not recover until he received her forgiveness. This could happen suddenly and without warning to Jack as a child, and continued to happen to Jack the self-confident and highly accomplished man, only now the mother was replaced by a wife. No wonder then that he left the women who could touch this wound, just as he had left his mother's home.

Again, giving attention and energy to his heart accelerated a healing process that had been going on his whole adult life. He set a personal record when his fourth marriage lasted as long as his first three marriages put together.

Inner, #2

> Design a rhythm for your day, week, month and year, and keep your rhythm. This conscious stability will allow your heart's capacity to increase.

There is a great power in arising in the morning at the time you have planned to arise; it is a power of the will that accrues to the heart.

When you make a schedule for the next day, you are acting as the master of your domain. You consider the needs of the morrow and you plan thoughtfully, starting with a time for waking and getting up. But when the time for awakening comes, the master is gone and the servant is present, who must carry out the plan left by the master the day before. It is the habit of the servant to grumble: "Why has the Master been so cruel? Don't I deserve more rest?" But the master is wiser than the servant, and if the Master's plan is not followed, something will be compromised or missed later in the day.

When you the servant obeys yourself the master, you energize the nobility of your being. The master in you is built up little by little, through every decision to honor the master over the servant. The result is that the servant part of yourself internalizes the master part and gains the power and wisdom of a master.

When you don't feel like meditating, the benefit of meditating is even greater. You demonstrate your commitment to your heart when you honor your practice time. You're not only practicing then, you're demonstrating your self-control and sense of priorities. It's like visiting a friend at the time you said you would call. Twenty minutes of practice at the time you scheduled is worth two hours of practice at a time that is convenient.

Heart Rhythm Meditation is specially designed to energize the heart. But doing the practice regularly has a further benefit: it establishes a rhythm for your day. People often tell us that they can't make time for meditation; their days are too full. However, if you set a time for it and do it at that time, it becomes a stake in the ground that your whole day revolves around. Everything else you have to do fits into the day nicely after that.

Energizing your heart is not a once-a-day thing; it needs to be done continually, so schedule time for it in your day, week, month and year. Daily, you can schedule a time for meditation, either in the morning, evening, or preferably both. In the middle of the day you'll also need a time to stop and reflect on what you're doing. Breaking the cycle of busyness is necessary to prevent yourself from going into automatic mode where you just react to events. Even if you have a job of repetitive transactions, you need some time to consider what you're doing, how it relates to larger goals, how you can do it better, and who you are. Then you can go back to the transactions with renewed energy in your heart.

In designing your rhythm, make time for both activity and relaxation, time alone and with others. There's always time for the urgent; you have to make time for the important.

8. Expanding the Inner Heart

Most people don't design a schedule; beyond a general time to start and stop work, to leave home and return home, to retire and awake, they just let the day unfold. But most people aren't consciously trying to energize the inner dimension of their hearts. You have to be responsive to the needs that arise -- you can't anticipate them all -- but you must also be determined to build a structure that can hold the demands of the day. Building the structure which is your schedule is analogous to building the container which is your heart. Your schedule needs a plan to hold its tasks; your heart needs a capacity to hold its love. Hold to a schedule and your heart will be strengthened.

Rabbi Zalman Schachter-Shalomi teaches about the many benefits of allocating a day per week to reflection, the joy of family and sacredness. A man asked him once how he could observe the Sabbath since his job required him to work on Saturday. The man was off on Wednesdays, so the Rabbi said, "Celebrate your Sabbath on Wednesday."

It's clearly easier to arrange time with your family on a day they also have available, so it makes sense for a family and a community to agree on their day of rest and worship. But if that's not possible, you still need a Sabbath sometime in the week.

On a monthly schedule, allocate a weekend per month to something that energizes your heart. What kinds of things energize your heart? You'll know afterward. On Monday morning, you can feel whether that weekend was depleting or energizing. If it was energizing, plan more of it next month.

Once a year, plan a week-long retreat. The great mystics of the past took 40 days per year for their retreats. In our culture that's very difficult, but you should be able to take 7 days together. What is a retreat? It's a time to do something different, to give balance to what you do the rest of the year, and it must be something you love to do. This time can feed you emotionally and spiritually for the whole year. Ideally, your retreat will take you to a new level of heart energy, making it possible for you to live from your heart in ways you've never done before.

Inner, #3

> Do not be concerned about protecting your open heart. What comes out of your heart has more impact upon you than what comes toward your heart.

We often hear the concern that people have about being able to live in the world with a heart that is open and sensitive. You will not have this problem if your heart is energized. The tendency to protect the heart, which everyone has learned to some extent, is a strategy of heart weakness. The wall that protects is also the wall that imprisons.

There is another kind of defense which allows you to remain open and receptive, and yet safe. This method is to be much more concerned with what comes out of you than what comes toward you.

It is not that which goes into the mouth that defiles one; but that which comes out of the mouth, this defiles one. -- Jesus Christ, Matthew 15:11

The best defense is a good offense.
-- *a paraphrase of George Washington, 1799.*

To understand this exercise, we need to understand individuality. An individual is like a bubble in an ocean. If a portion of the ocean is heated, some of the water will transform to water vapor, the gaseous version of the liquid water, and as this gas becomes concentrated in one area it will form a bubble within the water, surrounded by a boundary or membrane. Even though the water is transparent and the gas is transparent, the bubble can still be seen, due to the reflective quality of the bubble membrane. For some time this bubble, which is nothing more than water, seems to have a separate existence from the water around it, but eventually the bubble will be absorbed back into the ocean.

Whatever comes out of the individual strikes the bubble membrane and causes an echo within the bubble. This echo is the main factor determining the condition within the bubble; the bubble is mostly independent of the condition of the ocean. Yet the bubble is nothing more than ocean.

Therefore while you are always aware of your environment, your inner condition is mostly determined by your heart's response to the environment, not the environment itself.

> Bahá'u'lláh, the founder of the Bahá'í Faith, was imprisoned at `Akká, Palestine in 1868. A visitor reported that the prison conditions were atrocious. Without sanitation, the whole place reeked of human filth. Still, when the visitor was brought to the prisoner, Bahá'u'lláh welcomed him into his cell as if it were a palace. While they sat together, the great sage radiated such a peace that the prison was transformed into paradise.

While it is certainly true that people can be hurtful, and even your friends can be irritating, you'll find that the hurt coming toward you from others is mostly unconscious on their part. Their expression towards you has much more to do with their own heart than with yours. However, there is a grain of truth in every criticism. Find the grain of truth and leave the rest.

Consider what you can do to help the person who is being rude, critical, obstinate, or insulting. You have the opportunity to energize two hearts here.

The following is a story of short-term results from a woman who practices this Exercise for Life:

> The best thing is that I continue to feel more safe and able to be "out there" in the world. I am even doing things that I would not feel safe to do otherwise without Heart Rhythm Meditation, like talking to "strangers."
>
> I had to go for a blood test to a facility that I had not been to before. The person behind the counter at the office that I had gone to was being a combination of surly and rude. I stood at the counter for awhile waiting to have her acknowledge me so that I could find out the procedure of where to go and what to do. She continued on doing what she was doing without acknowledging me. Being ignored like that really bothers me, and I could feel the aggravation energy rising, so I thought of my heart and tried to send my voice from there as I said, "Hi."
>
> She fired back with a very aggravated and terse, "I will get to you when I'm done with this paperwork!"
>
> Un-offended, I replied, "I just wanted to say 'Hi,' please take your time." She melted, and a couple of seconds later connected with me, and asked if I was new to the office.
>
> Normally, I would have been the first to engage in, "Who can bite off whose head first." It was wonderful not to do that. What a difference! Thank you all for that contribution to an enormous change in how I communicate and express my fears and anxieties. I realized she was stressed and that I could help her by

being friendly instead of adding to the demands upon her.

Inner, #4

> Spend more time with people who recognize and admire you, and in nature. Make your environment beautiful and harmonious.

You create your environment, then you live within it, so it both expresses and affects your heart. This is called "heart ecology."

Why does this Exercise for Life energize the inner dimension of your heart? Because it follows the way the heart works. The heart is a collective faculty, not a private one. All beings are connected through the Heart of All, which they each reflect. When the heart is energized, it is comfortable with others and seeks to be present with others. The tendency to isolate oneself is a symptom of a wounded heart.

Those who admire you are the ones that recognize your greatness; they are the ones whose hearts are consciously connected to your own. Those who don't admire you are those who can't see their own likeness in you. Perhaps the dimensions of their hearts are so different from yours that they can't value your qualities. Those people can't energize you, although you could still energize them.

Nature appeals to every heart, and its energy helps restore the heart function. The Heart in nature is not covered by protection or defense, it is pure and simple, which is why nature can be so easily exploited. Wherever there is something wild, there is an energy that is regulated only by natural forces, not by man's design. This raw and uncompromised energy is material the heart needs to rebuild itself.

Beauty is found both in nature and in art, for the work of the artist is to make nature even more beautiful. Symmetry or balance of form, cleanness and clarity of line and harmony of color combine to make every expression of beauty. In these qualities, the heart finds its ideal: balance, clarity, and harmony, so naturally every heart is attracted to beauty. This Exercise for Life reminds us of this fact and connects the attraction of beauty to expanding the inner dimension of the heart.

In the development of the heart, we are concerned with the relation between the inner and outer world. Your heart projects itself into the world, and the state of your heart is seen in your environment. Conversely, the condition of your life affects your heart. As "ecology" is defined as the study of the relation between organisms and their environment, we call this relationship between a person's heart and their environment, "Heart Ecology." The heart ecologist, then, uses this principle of the double reflection of the world upon their heart and their heart upon the world. The heart ecologist makes a conscious effort to use those times when they feel their heart strongly to create their environment, so that their environment may return that impression of harmony and beauty when their heart is weaker.

In developing the inner dimension of the heart, you should avoid activities that use large amounts of heart energy for little consequence. One such activity is watching screens alone. We consider movies to be the greatest art form of our time, but they have one characteristic that makes them especially expensive for the inner dimension of the heart: the camera provides the viewer's point-of-view, and the camera can be cut quickly. In contrast, a play has one point-of-view determined by your seat in the audience.

Your heart is your true seat of identity, generating your point-of-view, but through the screen, your heart takes the point-of-view of the camera. In a fast-paced movie or television show where there are frequent visual cuts, each camera change challenges your point-of-view, requiring heart energy to readjust. In contrast, it is soothing to the heart to watch a scene from a constant point-of-view.

If you watch a movie with other people you can dialogue with, some of the energy required for mentally and emotionally processing the changing point-of-view is applied to a social function. But if you watch screens alone, there is no compensating social value.

There are many people who like to watch movies and television alone. If they have a strong inner dimension, they won't notice the depletion of their heart, but most people will feel the effects of it in further isolation from family and friends and less emotional power to accomplish what they want to accomplish. Greater passivity results from the diminished heart power. More and more stimulation will be necessary to keep a person's attention if their heart is weak, and this has caused the movie makers to make more camera cuts per minute. The number of cuts per minute in today's movies is an order of magnitude greater than 30 years ago, a sign that the practice is taking its toll on viewers' hearts.

Inner, #5

> Actively evoke surrender and glorification so that both of the great emotions become accessible to you.

What is the extent of your emotional range? If the inner dimension of your heart is weak, then you'll tend to avoid strong emotions of all kinds. If the inner dimension is strong, your heart will value grief, joy, anger, and all emotions, though they may be felt inwardly more than expressed outwardly. If you expose your heart to these emotions, they will stretch your heart into a larger container with a greater capacity for emotion.

At the opposite ends of the emotional range are the two great emotions of unconditional **surrender** and unbounded **glorification**. Surrender is your acceptance of the separation from wholeness which gave you individuality, and **glorification** is a celebration of that wholeness operating within you and through you.

These emotions are so large, they are cosmic; the sun, moon and planets dance to them, spinning in glorification while bowing to the gravitation that makes their paths bend in circles. These two great emotions interact to give rise to all the many variations of emotion we can feel.

You are probably much better at one of the great emotions than the other; everyone has their specialty, yet longs for the less familiar emotion. Powerful people seek out an opportunity to feel humbled and overwhelmed, as for example in religious rituals. Gentle people look for a relationship or situation that empowers them to express their hearts.

One sure way to gain access to profound emotion is by experiencing opera, classical music, blues, gospels, and many other kinds of music. Music touches the heart deeply, stimulating emotions that are always there but covered. Movies and drama are for most people even more effective in evoking emotion through the combination of music, dialogue and visuals.

Creating art is also an avenue to both surrender and glorification as the artist is humbled by the media and exalted by the act of creation.

We think the best way to evoke surrender and glorification is through relationships. Bowing to your beloved is easy and beautiful. Love says, "You are first; your happiness is my happiness." Then the smile of the beloved lifts the lover to ecstasy.

Harold is dedicated to his path of inner development and the discovery of the sacred spirit in all things. His search for the divine has taken him on numerous retreats, often long ones, alone. In his retreats he likes to get as close to nature as he can, and he practices surrender to the rhythm and elements of the natural world. He obeys the schedule of the sun, rising before sunrise and retiring into near-darkness after sunset. While it's light, he observes, reads and writes; while it's dark he reflects. He eats only local foods, either raw or cooked over a wood fire; he wears only natural fabrics. When walking, he tunes his pace to the speed of the wind.

His submission to nature is more important to him than his comfort. When it's cold, he has found he can let the cold pass right through him without resisting it. He imagines he is dispersing his body to let the winds blow through. When it's hot he yields to his body's ability to cool itself and drinks extra water. He celebrates the moon rise, the first drops of rain, the moment when the sun has dried the last drop on the big stone where he sits, and the visits of his bird and animal friends.

Harold's relationship with his wife of many years has become uninspiring to him. "I feel myself best when I am by myself," he says. He easily experiences the surrender and glorification of relating to nature; it is deeply emotional for him, but he rarely experiences the great emotions in his marriage.

Inspired by this Exercise for Life, Harold could see that the opportunities for surrender and glorification were abundant in the everyday life surrounding him, and especially in his relationship with his wife. Here was a startling thought: "Why do I value submission and joy in my relationship to nature more than in my relationship to my wife?" Well, "it's because nature is so impersonal," he replied to himself. But perhaps in a personal relationship he could make the great emotions even stronger than in nature.

He began an experiment: he would try to bring that same celebration that he felt at the visit of one of his nature friends to greeting his wife. He would consider harmony with her as important as harmony with the sun and moon. He would tune his rhythm to her energetic flows instead of tuning to the wind and rain. He would yield to her hot and cold moods as he did to the heat and coldness of nature. By doing this he felt he might find an even closer connection to the Heart of All that would reveal his own true self. Perhaps by practicing surrender and glorification in his relationship, he would be more himself with her than he could be alone.

Inner, #6

> Hold your emotion. Do not let yourself express your emotion in a personal way; that would vent it and deprive you of its power. Hold the emotion until it expresses itself in ways that are loving, harmonious and beautiful.

We see emotion as energy-in-motion and we delight in the wordplay of e-motion. The word "emotion" originated in the latin *emovere*, where "*e*" is short for "*ex*," meaning "out," and "*movere*" means "move." So the sense of movement has been in this word since Roman times. Emotion is an energy that moves out, out of the heart. When it does, its energy is released in expression. But if you do not express your emotion, you retain its emotional energy.

This way of working with emotion is nothing like repression, which comes from the idea that certain emotions are bad and should not be experienced. We value ALL emotions, for each emotion is energy in motion within the heart. Anger has its place and its power can be useful. You need to summon the power of anger if you want to overturn the tables of money changers in a sacred temple, for example. Grief is a part of life, and the grief of your mourners will be a testament to their love for you. Joy is highly prized, but rare. We think there are as many people afraid of their joy as are afraid of their sadness.

Most people live in a narrow middle range of emotions, avoiding the extremes of both positive and negative emotions. This avoidance is due partly to people's association of negative emotions with guilt and shame, and the positive emotions with intemperance and arrogance. We don't have these associations. Another part of the avoidance is due to the fear of being unable to control strong emotions. One imagines that if one can repress one's strong emotions, one can more easily control oneself. But repression doesn't work; repressed emotions inevitably surface in some way.

The path of the heart takes a different approach to emotions and their expression. Value all your emotions, but choose how to express them in ways that are loving, harmonious and beautiful. When you are aware of an emotion, you have an awareness of an internal energy. Feel it, value it, and let its power build to reveal its cause and purpose. Then choose how to use this power to create love, harmony and beauty.

Even if the emotion you feel is a "positive" one, still be careful how you express it. If, as soon as you feel affection, you exclaim, "I love you," the emotion never builds to a burning flame that consumes you. For the same reason, as soon as you say, "I hate you," you already feel better about the person. Any expression vents the emotion and reduces its power. The most powerful emotions cannot be expressed in words, for words distort and dilute the experience. It's better to hold the feeling and watch it mature and evolve.

Do not express glee, but hold the emotion until it becomes joy. Do not express anger, but hold it until it becomes powerful enough and focused enough to be harnessed. The objective is to be able to hold the truly great emotions, all at once, and then express them as some form of art.

Mike had a hard day at work, and returned home to find his family in an uproar. His young son was crying and his wife was at the end of her rope. They had moved into their home two months ago, but there were still unpacked boxes all over the living room. Unpacking got stalled because there was no room to put anything. Mike just wanted some peace and sympathy, but his wife had none to give. In her frustration, she complained bitterly. Mike was not responsive, so she turned up her volume and started in on him. He hadn't taken off enough time to get the house in order. How was she supposed to manage without help, she demanded. She succeed in getting Mike's attention as she blamed him for everything. Mike, still reeling from customers yelling at him all day, could feel the frustration, hurt and then anger building up in his chest. He was about to release his temper toward his wife when he remembered his Exercise for Life.

The way he picked up the hammer made his wife cringe, but he tucked it in his belt and picked up one of the heavy boards propped up against the wall in the living room. His muscles all tensing, he swung the board around and headed for the garage. He had meant to build the shelves for the wall, but every night he had been too tired by the time he got home. Tonight, with rage burning through his arteries, he had lots of energy. After several more trips, he had assembled the shelf material. Then he started the sanding. The physical effort soaked up his emotional energy and applied it to something he had put off doing. As the project progressed and the wood became more refined, Mike was becoming more refined too. Proudly, he brought the shelves into the living room and installed them, then filled them with the contents of the boxes, which he cut up and put in the trash. He had accomplished in an hour and a half what might have taken all day without the energy he had, and the living room looked great.

Jelaluddin Rumi wrote the Masvavi, his masterpiece of love poetry, in a state of bitter grief after the death of his beloved friend, Shams. Some 700 years later, it is the best selling poetry in the U.S. today.

Inner, #7

> Practice radiating peace from your heart like a force that brings everything it reaches into harmony and peace.

The base of all emotion is peace. Peace provides to every heart whatever emotion it is missing. The best way to experience peace is to radiate it.

When you dive into the depth of the heart, you descend through deeper and deeper layers of emotion that are less and less specific and yet building in intensity. It becomes more and more difficult to identify what emotion you're feeling, but the emotion is increasingly strong. This culminates in the discovery of a pool of pure emotion from which all emotions spring, deep in the bottom of your heart. We call that emotion "peace."

Conversely, as you ascend within the heart, you find a greater and greater variety of emotions which divide up the emotional power of the depth. This culminates at the surface of the heart, which we call the "mind." The mind has heard of emotion, but doesn't experience emotion itself.

You could say that the base of all emotions is love, but we don't consider love to be an emotion; it's a cosmic force that produces emotion, which is a flow of energy, in everything. When that energy is flowing between two people, it creates closeness, empathy, harmony, admiration and respect.

Peace is the base of all emotions the way white light is the base of all colors. The primary colors for light are red, green and blue. When you combine all the colors of light equally, the result in white light. In white light, all the colors are assimilated.[33] We see the emotion of peace as similar: peace is the combination of all emotions, and all emotions are assimilated within peace.

Some people think of peace as the absence of emotion. That is a transcendent kind of peace, a peace of the soul in another world, not here, not in the heart. There is a peace in the heart that is not transcendent, that is very much needed in

---

33 The situation is different in paint, where the mixture of all colors is black and the primary colors are red, yellow and blue.

this world, and that peace is a powerful and complete emotion.

The heart's peace radiates outward as a force that brings everyone it reaches into a state of harmony within themselves. It is like the way powerful waves from a passing boat obliterate the wind-driven ripples on the water. The waves of peace that emanate from a heart at peace, through the conscious breath, replace the waves of influence from outside and the waves of discontent from inside. As the waves of peace are absorbed by a person, their own heart is restored to the rhythmic harmony of peace.

You may question how it is that sending out waves of peace from the heart on the exhalation contributes to energizing the inner dimension of the heart. That question points up a mystery of the heart -- the energy of love within the heart is increased the more the energy is radiated outward. We don't know of a similar phenomenon in physics, that energy of any kind increases the more it is disbursed; that's the incredible nature of the heart.

Inner, #8

> Realize that you represent someone great. Your dedication will make all the qualities and power of the one you represent available to you in your heart.

None of us works alone; the universe is a network of beings, some visible and some not. Your thoughts are pulled from more general thoughts circulating throughout the network; your emotions are energies moving through your heart as they do through all hearts. You benefit from the experience of others, and your breakthroughs add to the net experience which is available to everyone. The more you are aware of this network of shared thoughts, emotions and experience, the better it works, for both the "uploads" and the "downloads."

When you can be aware of the specific people that you are representing, the transfer of their knowledge and inspiration is much more efficient. You recognize that you have had teachers, mentors and friends who have helped to form your current understanding and work. The next step is to recognize that you continue to represent these people and their knowledge and inspiration continues to flow through you, dynamically.

When you represent someone, you operate as an extension of that person into a space and time where they are not present. Initially, you represent your parents. Your body is literally an extension of their bodies. Your thinking is molded by their thinking -- most children accept the religious and political views of their parents, for example. And your parents see you as representing them, or at least they did when you were young, which is why your behavior reflects on them.

As an adult, you have been influenced by school teachers, bosses and friends, while you still retain the influence of your parents. Now you represent different people at different times. When relating to your spouse and children, you represent your parents. Even if you have developed a style of parenting quite different from your parents, you still represent them.

Speaking as grandparents, we can say we have delegated the raising of our grandchildren to their parents, who are well suited and motivated for the task. But if they died or became unable to raise their children, the responsibility would fall back on us, which we would accept.

At work, you represent your boss, the whole firm, and the interests of the shareholders. Your job is to do what benefits them.

On a grander scale, you represent the ones whom you choose to represent. If you have been moved by the life and teachings of Mahatma Gandhi, for example, then you may choose to represent him by extending his influence into the situations of your life, attempting to do in your time and place what he would do. By representing him, you may even extend his work into new areas and methods. Depending on the strength of your connection and how conscious your intention is, these extensions may be distortions or true developments of his work.

You may wish to represent a great man or woman of the past or present, but your ability to do so may be limited by the depth of your knowledge, the height of your realization, the breadth of your experience, and the power of your confidence. In the terms of this book, the dimensions of your heart may be insufficiently energized to enable you to fully represent the one you wish to represent. But your intention to do so has an effect; it causes dynamic inheritance to occur, in which the qualities of the heart of the person represented become reflected in your heart. This reflection develops and strengthens over time as you demonstrate your determination to put yourself aside and tune to the one you represent.

Paul was looking for a house to buy and was very interested in the one his realtor was showing him. The price and location were perfect, so he was excited to have a tour through the house. The realtor explained that it had an apartment that was presently rented on a month-to-month lease. As they knocked on the door of the apartment, the realtor went on to say that the tenant could be removed in time for the sale. They continued talking and knocking at the door, but there was no response.

As they walked away, the door sprang open and the tenant rushed out shouting, "You can't throw me out. I'm not leaving!" He caught up to Paul, who turned just before the tenant struck him in the face, knocking him to the floor.

As Paul rose to one knee he thought of the biblical Daniel, whose peace radiated so strongly that it calmed the lions. He stood up close to the tenant and faced the man calmly. "I'm not going to buy this house, but someone will, and I'm sorry if you're forced to move. I hope you find a place you like even better than this." The tenant, who had been shaking with anger, lowered his arms; his face softened and the anger drained out of him on the spot. He entered his apartment and shut the door. Paul thought, "Daniel helped me face my fear of being beaten up. I think he would have been pleased with my use of peace in real estate."

Developing the method of representation further, you may come to represent Jesus Christ, or even God. Whomever you represent, you inherit the qualities of their heart.

8. Expanding the Inner Heart

Chapter 9

Conclusion

9. Conclusion

The divine spirit, the soul of your soul, has projected itself through energy to be embodied in the matter of your body. At death your soul will withdraw itself from your body, but for now, your soul permeates every cell and is indivisible from its physical manifestation. The worlds of spirit, energy and matter are coexistent. The physical heart that circulates your blood is the same heart that continuously refreshes matter with spirit.

To put it another way, we can use the metaphor of light. There is a light that permeates the universe; the whole universe is made of it; you could call it "spirit." When that light collects itself in a spot, that spot is a soul, yet it is nothing but spirit. This light is perfectly pure. When the soul radiates its light through the space, it creates the appearance of a large sphere of light that obscures the soul in the center of the sphere, similar to the way a light appears in a fog. This sphere is the heart; it operates like the sun, which is also powered by an energy source within itself. The heart is a lamp; the soul is light itself. Without the heart, the light of the soul, which is of another dimension, would not be visible. The heart makes the soul's light, and all the qualities of that light, visible and operative in life.

The light of the heart is not uniform -- it has a size that varies in its different dimensions. As the light of the heart expands further, it creates additional spheres around itself; the next is the mind, the third and last is the body. These three spheres around the soul are nothing but light, but they may introduce patterns of lighter and darker light, and divide the sunlight of the heart into colors. So the physical heart is a projection of the energetic or emotional heart, which is itself nothing but a focus of the soul, a ray of the one spirit.

Just as spirit is ever changing, ebbing and flowing, your heart is changing constantly in its four dimensions. Sometimes it is expanding and strengthening, sometimes it is shrinking and weakening, as it responds to your intention, attention, inspiration, position, sensations and invocation, the six basic powers.

You can actively participate in the process of your heart's expansion by energizing your heart in one or more dimensions. You can do this by recognizing the dimensions of the heart in others, by practicing Heart Rhythm Meditation to focus the six basic powers on your heart, and by using the Exercises for Life to apply your heart in daily situations. As you do, your heart will respond like a sleeping giant awakened, and will come forward to guide and empower your life. Truly, a life with an energized heart is a beautiful life of love and service.

Appendix 1:
Exercises for Life

The Width of the Heart

If there is anyone with whom you would not like to be alone in an elevator, that is your signal that a reconciliation is needed, for the health of your own heart. Take the initiative to resolve your differences with that person so you do not have to fear them or be embarrassed by them. This will bring peace and contentment.

Mean what you say and say what you mean; speak clearly and simply. This will make you trustworthy.

When you give your word to someone, consider that you are bound to that person until they agree to release you from your commitment. This will make you dependable.

Look at things from another person's point-of-view. Your own point-of-view will not be lost, but your view of reality will be widened.

When the lack of focus, initiative, persistence or success of others around you annoys you, take this as a signal that you need to improve your own self-mastery through concentration on some specific, personal goal.

Consider what is expected of you by all those with whom you come in contact and try to answer their demands to the best of your ability, willingly, and patiently. Give something to each person, as generously as possible, choosing the level at which you give: physically, mentally, emotionally, or spiritually.

When you possess something, think of the one who does not possess it. This will make you considerate and thankful.

Identify yourself with someone else, to remove the assumptions you make about who you must be and what role you must play. Try thinking of yourself as a teacher, an animal, a leader, a man, a woman, a humble saint, etc. In this way you will come to appreciate the qualities and strengths of others, and gain them for yourself.

The Depth of the Heart

See yourself reflected in another. See how that person is similar to you. See how they become more similar as you feel more accommodation, respect, admiration and love for them.

Feel another person. People are very different than they appear and even different than they think they appear. Your feeling of another tells you more than their words and actions can.

Identify what irritates you about yourself when you see it reflected in another. Recognize that it is your own emerging quality you see in the one you admire.

Practice forgiveness, thereby demonstrating how the heart operates most naturally. Forgiveness can be practiced as tolerance, overlooking, and forgetting.

Reveal your innermost being with dignity; by so doing, you teach others how the heart operates.

Let your heart be moved by the beauty and tragedy all around you.

Don't avoid emotional pain; instead, experience your heart's pain with all your awareness, until it becomes a physical sensation. Go so deeply into pain that it becomes the pain of humanity. Let the pain turn to joy, to all feeling.

Forget the errors of others. Your reproach may make them more resolved in their faults. Do not dwell on your own errors either. People are seldom improved by guilt. Blame no one for anything. Rather, try to understand their reason.

The Height of the Heart

Optimism is your natural condition; optimism comes from love. Consider pessimism to be a warning sign of a weakened heart.

Regret is a waste of energy. The past has given you the present that will be opened in the future. Be resigned to the past, attentive to the present and hopeful for the future.

Pursue happiness, not only pleasure. Make time for the important, not only the urgent.

Hold fast to your high regard for others; don't let their weaknesses lower your opinion of them. Look for the best in people and they will come up to your estimation of them.

Take the worst part of something and transform it so it becomes the best part, whether you are renovating your business, home or personality.

Uphold your honor at any cost. Hold your ideal high in all circumstances. You may fail to live up to your ideal, but never lower your ideal to the height of your ability.

Do not take advantage of a person's ignorance. Seek not pleasure through the pain of another, life through the death of another, gain through the loss of another, nor honor through the humiliation of another. Influence no one to do wrong.

Do nothing which will make your conscience feel guilty. A clear conscience gives the strength of a lion, but a guilty conscience can turn a lion into a rabbit.

The Forward Dimension of the Heart

Feel the wish of your heart, that which your heart has wished for all your life, and still desires.

Become passive with respect to the power of the heart within you.

Do something every day toward the accomplishment of your heart's wish.

Have more effect upon the world than the world has upon you.

Consider every problem as a challenge to the power of your creativity.

You can have whatever your heart wants most. Indeed, the path to its attainment is already prepared for you. It is your birthright that has created your desire.

Do not spare yourself in the work which you must accomplish.

Once you have allowed a wish into your heart, you must accomplish it. The only exception is when you grow beyond it, like a child outgrowing his toys.

The Inner Dimension of the Heart

Throughout the day, keep your heart energized by touching your heart with the energy of your breath and placing your attention on your heartbeat.

Design a rhythm for your day, week, month and year, and keep your rhythm. This conscious stability will allow your heart's capacity to increase.

Do not be concerned about protecting your open heart. What comes out of your heart has more impact upon you than what comes toward your heart.

Spend more time with people who recognize and admire you, and in nature. Make your environment beautiful and harmonious.

Actively evoke surrender and glorification so that both of the great emotions become accessible to you.

Hold your emotion. Do not let yourself express your emotion in a personal way; that would vent it and deprive you of its power. Hold the emotion until it expresses itself in ways that are loving, harmonious and beautiful.

Practice radiating peace from your heart like a force that brings everything it reaches into harmony and peace.

Realize that you represent someone great. Your dedication will make all the qualities and power of the one you represent available to you in your heart.

Appendix 2:
The Teachings of Hazrat Inayat Khan

Hazrat Inayat Khan (1883-1927) was an Indian musician and sage who lectured in the United States and Europe on the unity of all religions, presenting a comprehensive method of developing the heart. His teachings form the single most important influence to our work in the Institute for Applied Meditation and the material in this book and in *Living from the Heart*.

IAM has created an online database of Hazrat Inayat Khan's teaching so that it can be easily accessed and studied. All the references in this book to his teachings can be located through this website, located at www.hazrat-inayat-khan.org.

The system of referencing used in this book for Hazrat Inayat Khan's lectures and poetry is designed to make it easy to find on this website. For example, the quote:

Rocks will open and make way for the lover.

This quote is referenced as:

www.hazrat-inayat-khan.org: Message: Complete Works: Sayings: Gayan: Boulas.

Appendix 2: The Teachings of Hazrat Inayat Khan

Appendix 3:
The Institute for Applied Meditation

IAM is a non-profit spiritual school that develops and applies Heart Rhythm Meditation for integrating physical, emotional and spiritual life to consciously create love, harmony and beauty.

IAM offers courses in meditation, mentoring, teaching, and healing that draw on the methods of the great mystics of all traditions for opening, healing, listening to, energizing and applying the spiritual heart in life.

IAM offers an initiatic path, in the lineage of Hazrat Inayat Khan, through all the stages of mystical experience leading to the illuminated heart in service to God and humanity.

More information about IAM can be found at:

www.applied-meditation.org

Appendix 3: The Institute for Applied Meditation

References

Allison, T. G., D. E. Williams, et al. (1995). "Medical and economic costs of psychologic distress in patients with coronary artery disease". *Mayo Clinic Proceedings* 70(8): 734-742.

Antonovsky, A. (1987). *Unraveling the Mystery of Health: How People Manage Stress and Stay Well*. San Francisco, Jossey-Bass.

Armour, J. A. (1991). "Anatomy and function of the intrathoracic neurons regulating the mammalian heart". In: I. H. Zucker and J. P. Gilmore, eds. *Reflex Control of the Circulation*. Boca Raton, FL, CRC Press. 1-37.

Armour, J. A. and J. Ardell, Eds. (1994). *Neurocardiology*. New York, NY, Oxford University Press.

Bair, Puran. (1998) *Living from the Heart*. New York: Three Rivers Press.

Bair, Puran. (2007) "Visible Light Radiated from the Heart with Heart Rhythm Meditation". *Subtle Energies and Energy Medicine*. 16(3): 211-215

Barks, Coleman, trans. 2002. *The Soul of Rumi*. New York: Harper Collins.

Barrios-Choplin, B., R. McCraty, et al. (1997). "An inner quality approach to reducing stress and improving physical and emotional wellbeing at work". *Stress Medicine* 13: 193-201.

Barrios-Choplin, B., R. McCraty, et al. (1999). "Impact of the HeartMath self-management skills program on physiological and psychological stress in police officers". Boulder Creek, CA, HeartMath Research Center, *Institute of HeartMath*, Publication No. 99-075.

Cantin, M. and J. Genest. (1986). "The heart as an endocrine gland". *Clinical and Investigative Medicine* 9(4): 319-327.

Carroll, D., G. Smith, et al. (1998). "Blood pressure reactions to the cold pressor test and the prediction of ischaemic heart disease: data from the Caerphilly Study". *Journal of Epidemiology and Community Health* (Sept.): 528-529.

Childre, D. (1998). Freeze-Frame: One Minute Stress Management. Boulder Creek, CA, Planetary Publications.

Childre, D. and H. Martin (1999). The HeartMath Solution. San Francisco, HarperSanFrancisco.

Damasio, A. R. (1994). *Descartes' Error: Emotion, Reason and the Human Brain*. NY, G.P. Putnam's Sons.

Elliott, W.J., H.R. Black, A. Alter, B. Gavish. (2004) "Blood pressure reduction with device-guided breathing: pooled data from 7 controlled studies." *Journal of Hypertension*; 22(2): S116.

Elliott, W., J Izzo, Jr., WB White, D Rosing, CS Snyder, A Alter, B Gavish, HR Black. (2004) "Graded Blood Pressure Reduction in Hypertensive Outpatients Associated with Use of a Device to Assist with Slow Breathing." *Journal of Clinical Hypertension*; 6(10): 553-559.

Fredrickson, B. (1998). "What good are positive emotions?" *Review of General Psychology* 2(3): 300-319.

Gahery, Y. and D. Vigier (1974). "Inhibitory effects in the cuneate nucleus produced by vago-aortic afferent fibers". *Brain Research* 75: 241-246.

Goleman, D. (1995). *Emotional Intelligence*. NY, Bantam Books.

Grossarth-Maticek, R., H. J. Eysenck, et al. (1988). "Personality type, smoking habit and their interaction as predictors of cancer and coronary heart disease". *Personality and Individual Differences* 9(2): 479-495.

Grossarth-Maticek, R. and H. J. Eysenck (1991). "Creative novation behaviour therapy as a prophylactic treatment for cancer and coronary heart disease: Part I–Description of treatment; Part II–Effects of treatment". *Behaviour Research and Therapy* 29(1): 1-16; 17-31.

Grossarth-Maticek, R. and H.J. Eysenck (1995). "Self-regulation and mortality from cancer, coronary heart disease and other causes: A prospective study". *Personality and Individual Differences* 19(6): 781--795.

Grossman, E., Grossman, A., Schein MH, Zimlichman R, Gavish B. 2001. "Breathing-control lowers blood pressure." *Journal of Human Hypertension*. Apr; 15(4):263-269.

Institute of HeartMath. (2001). The Science of the Heart. Boulder Creek, HeartMath Research Center, Institute of HeartMath, Publication No. 01-001.

Johari, Harish. (2000) *Chakras: Energy Centers of Transformation*. Destiny Books. Revised edition.

Joseph, Chacko N., Cesare Porta, Gaia Casucci, Nadia Casiraghi, Mara Maffeis, Marco Rossi and Luciano Bernardi. 2005. "Slow breathing improves arterial baroflex sensitivity and decreases blood pressure in essential hypertension." *Hypertension*. 2005: 46, 714-718.

Khan, Pir Vilayat Inayat. (1983) *Leader's Manual*. New Lebanon, NY: Sufi Order International.

Kübler-Ross, Elizabeth. (1969) *On Death and Dying*. New York: MacMillan.

Lacey, J. I. and B. C. Lacey (1978). Two-way communication between the heart and the brain: Significance of time within the cardiac cycle. *American Psychologist* (February): 99-113.

LeDoux, J. (1996). *The Emotional Brain: The Mysterious Underpinnings of Emotional Life*. New York, Simon and Schuster.

Luskin, F., M. Reitz, et al. (2000). Pilot study of a group stress management training on elderly patients with congestive heart failure. *Journal of Cardiopulmonary Rehabilitation* 20(5): 303.

Malik, M. and A. J. Camm, Eds. (1995). *Heart Rate Variability.* Armonk, NY: Futura Publishing Company.

McCraty, R., M. Atkinson, et al. (1996). Music enhances the effect of positive emotional states on salivary IgA. *Stress Medicine* 12: 167-175.

McCraty, R., M. Atkinson, et al. (1995). The effects of emotions on short term heart rate variability using power spectrum analysis. *American Journal of Cardiology* 76: 1089-1093.

McCraty, R., M. Atkinson, et al. (1996). The Electricity of Touch: Detection and measurment of cardiac energy exchange between people. Proceedings of the Fifth Appalachian Conference on Neurobehavioral Dynamics: Brain and Values, Radford VA, Lawrence Erlbaum Associates. Mahwah, NJ.

McCraty, R., W. A. Tiller, et al. (1996). Head-heart entrainment: A preliminary survey. Proceedings of the Brain-Mind Applied Neurophysiology EEG Neurofeedback Meeting, Key West, Florida.

McCraty, R. and A. Watkins (1996). Autonomic Assessment Report: A Comprehensive Heart Rate Variability Analysis – Interpretation Guide and Instructions. Boulder Creek, CA, Institute of HeartMath.

McCraty, R., B. Barrios-Choplin, et al. (1998). The effects of different music on mood, tension, and mental clarity. *Alternative Therapies in Health and Medicine* 4(1): 75-84.

McCraty, R., B. Barrios-Choplin, et al. (1998). The impact of a new emotional self-management program on stress, emotions, heart rate variability, DHEA and cortisol. *Integrative Physiological and Behavioral Science* 33(2): 151-170.

McCraty, R., M. Atkinson, et al. (1999). The impact of an emotional self-management skills course on psychosocial functioning and autonomic recovery to stress in middle school children. Integrative Physiological and Behavioral Science 34(4): 246-268.

McCraty, R. and M. Atkinson (1999). Influence of afferent cardiovascular input on cognitive performance and alpha activity. Proceedings of the Annual Meeting of the Pavlovian Society, Tarrytown, NY.

McCraty, R., M. Atkinson, et al. (1999). The role of physiological coherence in the detection and measurement of cardiac energy exchange between people. Proceedings of the Tenth International Montreux Congress on Stress, Montreux, Switzerland.

McCraty, R. (1999). The Freeze-Framer: A stress management training and heart rhythm education system for increasing physiological coherence. Proceedings of the Tenth International Montreux Congress on Stress, Montreux, Switzerland.

McCraty, R. (2000). Psychophysiological coherence: A link between positive emotions, stress reduction, performance and health. Proceedings of the Eleventh International Congress on Stress, Mauna Lani Bay, Hawaii.

McCraty, R., M. Atkinson, et al. (2001). Analysis of twenty-four hour heart rate variability in patients with panic disorder. Biological Psychology: In press.

Meles, E., C Giannattasio, M Failla, G Gentile, A Capra, G Mancia. (2004) "Nonpharmacologic Treatment of Hypertension by Respiratory Exercise in the Home Setting." American Journal of Hypertension; 17:370-374.

Murphy, D. A., G. W. Thompson, et al. (2000). The heart reinnervates after transplantation. Annals of Thoracic Surgery 69(6): 1769-1781.

Nixon, P. G. F. (1976) The human function curve. Practitioner 217: 765-769; 935-944.

Paddison, S. (1998). The Hidden Power of the Heart: Discovering an Unlimited Source of Intelligence. Boulder Creek, CA, Planetary Publications.

Parati G, Izzo JL Jr, Gavish B., Third Edition. JL Izzo and HR Black, Eds. (2003) "Respiration and Blood Pressure." *Hypertension Primer*, Ch. A40, p117-120.

Pearson, T. D., E. Rapaport, et al. (1994). Optimal risk factor management in the patient after coronary revascularization: a statement for healthcare professionals from an American Heart Association writing group. AHA Medical/Scientific Statement. Circulation 90: 3125-3133.

Rein, G., M. Atkinson, et al. (1995). The physiological and psychological effects of compassion and anger. *Journal of Advancement in Medicine* 8(2): 87-105.

Rosenfeld, S. A. (1977). Conversations Between Heart and Brain. Mental Health Studies and Reports Branch, Division of Scientific and Public Information, National Institute of Mental Health, Rockville, MD.

Rosenthal, T., Alter A, Peleg E, Gavish B. (2001) "Device-guided breathing exercises reduce blood pressure - Ambulatory and home measurements." American Journal of Hypertension; 14:74-76.

Rozman, D., R. Whitaker, et al. (1996). A pilot intervention program which reduces psychological symptomatology in individuals with human immunodeficiency virus. Complementary Therapies in Medicine 4: 226-232.

Sandman, C. A., B. B. Walker, et al. (1982). Influence of afferent cardiovascular feedback on behavior and the cortical evoked potential. In: J. Cacioppo, J. T. and R. E. Petty, eds. *Perspectives in Cardiovascular Psychophysiology*. New York, The Guilford Press.

Schein M, Gavish B, Herz M, Rosner-Kahana D, Naveh P, Knishkowy B, Zlotnikov E, Ben-Zvi N, Melmed RN. (2001) "Treating hypertension with a device that slows and regularizes breathing: A randomised, double-blind controlled study." Journal of Human Hypertension; 15:271-278.

Siegman, A. W., S. T. Townsend, et al. (1998). Dimensions of anger and CHD in men and women: self-ratings versus spouse ratings. Journal of Behavioral Medicine 21(4): 315-336.

Swank, R. and W. Marchand (1946). Combat neuroses. Archives of Neurology and Psychiatry 55: 236-247.

Thomas, S. A., E. Friedmann, et al. (1997). Psychological factors and survival in the cardiac arrhythmia suppression trial (CAST): a reexamination. American Journal of Critical Care 6(2): 116-126.

Tiller, W., R. McCraty, et al. (1996). "Cardiac coherence; A new non-invasive measure of autonomic system order". Alternative Therapies in Health and Medicine 2(1): 52-65.

Umetani, K., D. H. Singer, et al. (1998). "Twenty-four hour time domain heart rate variability and heart rate: relations to age and gender over nine decades". Journal of the American College of Cardiology 31(3): 593-601.

Viskoper, R, Shapira, I, Priluck, R, Mindlin, R, Chornia, L, Laszt, A, Dicker, D, Gavish, B, Alter, A. (2003) "Non-Pharmacological Treatment of Resistant Hypertensives by Device-Guided Slow Breathing Exercises." American Journal of Hypertension; 16:484-487.

Washington, George (1989) Rules of Civility and Decent Behavior in Company and Conversation. Applewood Books. Also available at: http://www.foundationsmag.com/civility.html

Watkins, A., Ed. (1997). Mind-Body Medicine: A Clinician's Guide to Psychoneuroimmunology. London, Churchill Livingstone.

Watkins, A. D. (1995). Perceptions, emotions and immunity: an integrated homeostatic network. Quarterly Journal of Medicine 88: 283-294.

Index

SPECIAL OFFER

Go deeper into the heart!

Send us your proof of purchase (plus $3.49 shipping and handling) and receive a **FREE** meditation CD.

This remarkable CD provides you with step-by-step meditation instruction based on the principles in *Energize Your Heart*.

Send this form with your check or money order for $3.49 to:

Institute for Applied Meditation
P.O. Box 86149, Tucson, AZ, 85754

Name——————————————————————

Address—————————————————————

Telephone————————————————————

email ——————————————————————

Occupation————————————————————

☐ I'd like to pay the $3.49 with my credit card:

Card #——————————————— Exp———

☐ Yes, I'd like to receive emails from IAM about the power and beauty of the heart! (We do not share emails with anyone)

☐ No emails please.

Limit One (1) CD per household. Offer good while supplies last.